The Internet

FOR BEGINNERS

Laurel Brunner and Zoran Jevtic

Edited by Richard Appignanesi

ICON BOOKS

Published in 1997 by Icon Books Ltd.,
Grange Road, Duxford, Cambridge CB2 4QF
e-mail: icon@mistral.co.uk

Reprinted 1997

Distributed in the UK, Europe, Canada, South Africa and Asia
by the Penguin Group:
Penguin Books Ltd., 27 Wrights Lane, London W8 5TZ

Published in Australia in 1997 by Allen & Unwin Pty. Ltd.,
PO Box 8500, 9 Atchison Street, St. Leonards, NSW 2065

Originating editor: Richard Appignanesi

ISBN 1 874166 84 6

Printed and bound in Great Britain by
Biddles Ltd., Guildford and King's Lynn

Welcome to the Internet

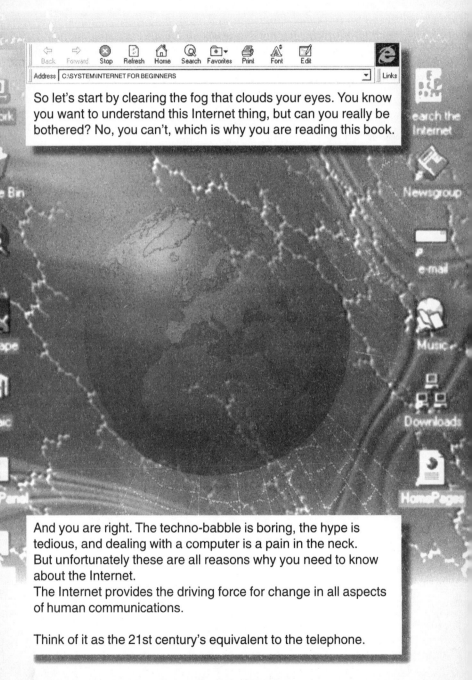

Address C:\SYSTEM\INTERNET FOR BEGINNERS

So let's start by clearing the fog that clouds your eyes. You know you want to understand this Internet thing, but can you really be bothered? No, you can't, which is why you are reading this book.

And you are right. The techno-babble is boring, the hype is tedious, and dealing with a computer is a pain in the neck.
But unfortunately these are all reasons why you need to know about the Internet.
The Internet provides the driving force for change in all aspects of human communications.

Think of it as the 21st century's equivalent to the telephone.

What is the Internet?

The Internet is not a tangible object that you can reach out and touch. The Internet is a cooperative organic entity, the digital parallel of human experience, capable of reaching and serving all manner of information and interests, from research into carbon structures to horse-racing. It provides electronic tools such as software, music, images, multimedia, video, text, and a cheap way to turn long distance communications into local phone calls. But unlike the phone, which is a one-at-a-time circuit-switched system, the Internet provides dynamic and open connections with many people at once.

Whatever you can think of, there will be a group of people with similar interests to talk things over with.

There will be a site with bucket-loads of information for you to peruse.

Knowledge is power – which is why the Internet casts such an intoxicating spell.

The concept of the Internet alone can boggle the mind into stupefaction. But take heart, and don't think of the Internet as an infinity to conquer. Think of it as a cheap way to send letters, an easy way to book theatre tickets, and a hassle-free means of getting the best deal.

45 to 50% off what something costs in normal shops can be well worth the trouble.

It seems complicated because it has evolved over a long period of time and has many, many components, all of which are still evolving.

ardware

information

upgrades

freebies

music files

graphics

multimedia

interconnecti

The Internet is a layered complexity of technologies and services that have gradually come together to form something everyone can share. Internet culture is characterized by openness and lack of commercial imperative. It is a never-ending structure, pragmatic, free and impossible to constrain.

sounds

animations

interaction

education

shopping

46" HRF

144" HF

But there are issues to consider before you leap into the digital void. Most important of these is TIME. The Internet is an amazing community of people. Scientists, computer programmers, government organizations, political parties, self-help groups, people with disabilities, clothes-designers, artists, musicians and anything else you can think of.

This means you can have conversations, arguments, be nosey, rude, loving, sarcastic, provocative, anything you like to anyone you like, under any guise you like.

This is fine if you have a lonely life or are bored.

Amazing though this is, it takes you away from anything else you might be doing, or should be doing.

Not fine if you have other people who want to be with you.

If you fit into the latter category, plan your time and consider your social responsibilities. Time, unlike the Internet, is not infinite in the ordinary world of the average little farty person.

Remember that like knowledge, language too is power, and the language of the Internet and computing worlds can be very difficult to digest if you like your language plain. As with any form of communication, you need to know the language to communicate well, but you can probably get by with knowing a little.

There is a vast array of terminologies, acronyms and abbreviations that will confuse you. The Internet has a lexicon all its own. Once you understand its point and purpose, you will find that the lexicon is far from intimidating.

> Actually, a lot of the words bandied about by Internet and computing aficionados are either misused, misapplied or utterly irrelevant to the conversation.

> People can't resist showing off, especially where digital technology is concerned.

ISP GIF modem e-mail VIRUS BAUD node script off-line hyper ASCII @.com TCP/IP access ActiveX foru JPG http:// class SEARCH bookm DNS ftp server ethernet MIME WYSIWYG Java brows HTML BMP

Most of the language of the Internet describes a digital and abstracted equivalent of what we already do and have done for years in the analogue world: **communicate**. The Internet is the ultimate digital communications system.

So what makes digital systems special? Well, digital computers use only two states, **on** or **off** (electrically charged or not), to control and effect incredibly complex processes. A digital computer works with information broken down into discrete elements or binary digits (otherwise known as **bits**) that are expressed as a series of electrical pulses. Binary digits or bits are expressed using only two numbers, 0 and 1 (on or off, see). Because they are the simplest form of numerical expression, they are the basis of binary codes. These codes can be built up into sets of incredibly complicated processes using programming languages made up of various language-specific commands and instructions.

The efficiency with which a program runs depends on the suitability of a programming language for a given task, how well written the instructions are, and on the electronics in the computer. Thus the more powerful the microprocessor (the microprocessor is the computer's brain), the more data-processing power you have, because the more binary code it can munch through.

Think of it as a sort of engine: the more powerful the engine, the greater the load it can move.

In a computer, the more binary code you can process, the greater the complexity of the information and the speed with which it can be handled.

Bits are combined into larger eight-bit entities called **bytes**, basically to make them more manageable. There's an internationally agreed set of one-byte binary codes that match letters, the **ASCII** standard (the American Standard Code for Information Interchange) – a set of basic alphanumeric codes and the foundation for computing. Letters form words, words form sentences or instructions that tell the computer what to do. Computer languages are used to create sets of instructions or programs dedicated to doing a particular thing – such as word-processing, calculating tricky sums, or sending messages across the Internet.

An operating system is a very powerful suite of computer programs that work together to control the actual computer itself.

In the early days of computing, each computer had its own operating system, which was why linking two together was such a problem and why networks of computers were not easy to build.

About Networks

A network connects collections of like-minded entities together. A network of friends who play tennis, a network of trains, of rivers, tunnels, shipping lanes, telephone lines, electrical wires or people. You can link different sorts of networks together to create an extended networked system. For example, ferries take road traffic across and along rivers, trains and ocean liners can carry cars from one stretch of road to another, and a network of tennis enthusiasts can extend their numbers by inviting the local speleology club to a friendly match.

No matter how small or how specific they are, two separate networks linked by some common interest together form an **internetworked** system.

Even though tennis-players and troglodytes are different, they can share two disparate worlds because they agree to communicate on the basis of a common interest. The national telephone system connects to other national telephone systems to create an international telephone network. Such networks are then interlinked or internetworked.

An electronic system is made up of separate digital components strung together with wires and cables. Two electronic systems such as your CD player and radio amplifier or television and video (or all four of them) can be linked over cables that carry signals that the different elements can understand.

We have wires everywhere, lots of them doing all sorts of things.

But wires can't do anything except carry electrical signals, like a pipe carries water or a road carries traffic. Directions of flow can be changed, journeys can be rerouted or diverted, content can be checked, and so on, but something has to do this, like traffic lights or reservoirs. In the digital world, computers direct the flow and are the checkpoints that control and oversee the traffic.

And computers are the source and destinations for the data journeys.

One of the clever things about networked systems is that you can use the resources or services available on the network. There's nothing new in this idea. You can call any internetworked system an internet, but "The Internet" is very specific. It is the internetworked system for *worldwide communications* made up of telephone lines and computer networks of all kinds. These linked networks turn into an *inter*network because of common unifying factors which allow the various networks to cooperate.

Everything they do is ultimately either described digitally or is converted into a digital form.

And they all follow certain codes of conduct, rules of digital behaviour.

In the early days of the Internet, computer programmers wanted to be able to share activities, initially using computing resources located elsewhere, but later using knowledge resources. Once they had the means to link the machines, they developed the means for accessing and using those remote computers. Then they started swapping information, first as simple electronic mail messages, then on a larger scale sharing research material, software programs and so on.

So who started it? A collection of people all working on different things who came together to share work and to solve a particular problem.

In the 1960s, the American Department of Defense funded a research group called the Advanced Research Projects Agency (ARPA). There was a healthy respect for the value of scientific research, and lots of money about.

The Cold War, Sputnik and a general atmosphere of paranoia meant that scads of public dollars were thrown at all sorts of ARPA whimsies. One of these was a networking project that would link very powerful purpose-built computers together, so that academic and research establishments could share them.

The idea came about because computers were extremely difficult and expensive to build.

And at that time, people used dumb terminals to access the computer on a time-share basis.

The networking project was intended to make remote computing resources available to a range of sites, thereby increasing the availability of powerful computers within the computer science community.

14

The stuff about the origins of the Internet being to provide device redundancy isn't really true, although obviously distributed data systems are less vulnerable than centralized ones.

The incredibly generous funding by ARPA was the key to the development of the original networked system, which cost a fortune to develop and run. Later, yet more generous funding, this time by the National Science Foundation, had the effect of ultimately democratizing an array of diverse technologies. An appreciation of the communications potential of internetworked systems then led rapidly to the development of common modes of operation and to viable standards that other networked systems could use.

> Long long ago, each computer built was designed and made almost as a one-off.

> There were no standard operating systems or data formats.

> Your computer terminal was merely a window into a vast beast that grumbled away somewhere else.

> ARPA research contractors set out to design and build a machine that could sit between the computer and a telephone line, like this.

Computer + IMP + PHONE LINE + IMP + Computer

The IMPs (Interface Message Processors) were dedicated communications machines that bridged a computer and the telephone lines connecting remote locations.

The first IMP was installed at the University of California at Los Angeles (UCLA) in September 1969, and the second at Stanford Research Institute (SRI) in northern California a couple of months later.

By the end of 1969 there were four connected sites – UCLA, SRI, UCSB (University of California at Santa Barbara), and the University of Utah – and the ARPANet was born.

Over time, the ARPANet evolved and added new sites, with users coming up with ideas for its use. The ARPA group name changed to Defense Advanced Research Projects Agency in 1970, and over the next fifteen years the network grew steadily.

The idea of linking computer networks came about because people wanted to share information on a wider scale.

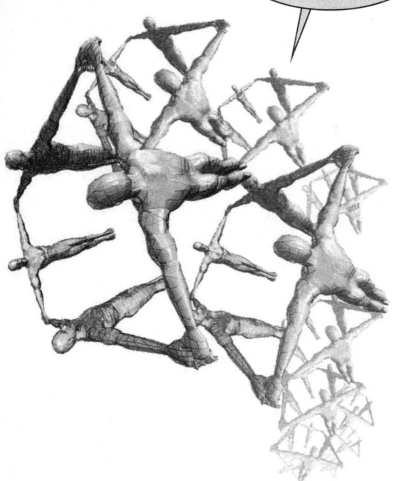

There were several networks: ARPANet (the one invented for ARPA), JANet (the Joint Academic Network, superseded by SuperJANet) which linked UK universities, and most importantly NSFNet, built by the American National Science Foundation. Crucially, they followed the design principles and protocols of the ARPANet.

In 1985 the National Science Foundation agreed to build a network called
NSFNet, linking five supercomputers in the United States to provide
scientists of all kinds with a means of connecting to the Internet. Local
communities could then connect to this backbone network and each other.
By 1983, the ARPANet had grown huge, and all networked computer
systems followed common protocols.

Security was
a worry, so the
Department of Defense
sliced the network
into two.

It kept the secret
stuff on MilNet and left the
remainder to continue
to evolve.

This was the basis of the Internet, although by the end of 1989 the
original creaking network was switched off, outpaced by the newer, fleeter
NSFNet and others.

Packet Switching

Separately, in the 60s at the University of Sussex, **packet switching** was proposed as a means of moving data. This technique breaks up data into discrete data packets which are then routed to their destination. The packets travel using the most efficient route available and do not necessarily travel together. They are reassembled at their destination, recreating their original data set. Packet switching is a means of moving data between digital devices without an established communication path.

This development paralleled work underway elsewhere in the US.

It was the foundation of another key component of the Internet, because it uses a routing **algorithm**, a set of rules or process instructions, to get message parts to where they are supposed to go.

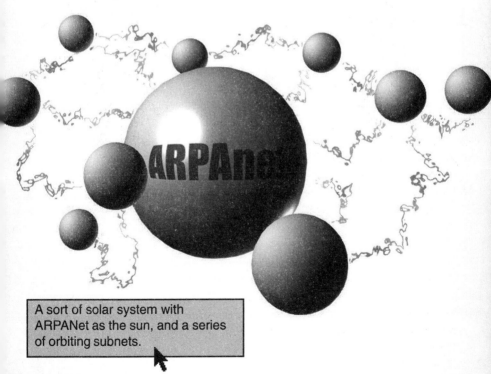

A sort of solar system with ARPANet as the sun, and a series of orbiting subnets.

There were also developments underway in networking technology. Ethernet linked computers on local and wide area networks and so made it much easier to connect them. The invention of Ethernet created an enormous community of network-users who for the first time didn't have to be engineers to get their computers to work in a networked environment.

Remote Ethernet local area networks (LANs) at universities were able to use ARPANet hubs to connect to other remote LANs at universities thousands of miles away.

This was a vital advance in the evolution of the Internet.

Ethernet was invented to create a means of sharing computing resources within a building.

But the model was easily extended to link computer networks at different sites.

Ethernet is a LAN protocol developed by Xerox Corporation in cooperation with DEC and Intel in 1976.

The invention spawned a host of new business opportunities from cables to routers, and network black boxes of all kinds.

The Unix Operating System and SUN

The development of the multi-tasking Unix operating system, as a basis for open non-proprietary systems, was another crucial development in the evolution of the Internet. Its widespread adoption was the basis of open systems. If a computer could run the highly adaptable Unix operating system, it could easily be linked to other computers running Unix.

Besides being the second site on the ARPANet, Stanford University also produced the founders of SUN Microsystems.

21

The Ethernet-SUN-Unix triumvirate gave the Internet major momentum because it provided the key components for a cooperative distributed digital system of data interchange. And significantly, these technologies were available to ordinary mortals beyond the hallowed halls of the computer science community.

Commercial imperatives encouraged widespread evangelizing of these and similar but compatible technologies for general computing and business.

This meant that the tools for widespread internetworking were soon in place throughout the commercial and academic worlds.

There were also developments in commercial bulletin board services, which provided people with a computer-based discussion forum and covered a wide range of specific interests, from developments in particle physics to the effects of excess sun. These dedicated commercial services did not use the same data transport protocols as other networks, but they provided a communications method that soon became very popular.

Bulletin board services, now known as **online services**, provided people with a means to communicate using computers.

CompuServe is the oldest and best-known of these.

To this day, many of these online services still use their own protocols and work with Internet protocols to provide a gateway onto the Internet.

Some of the bulletin board services did choose to follow ARPANet's conventions, and have evolved into the newsgroups that now populate the Internet in such abundance.

TCP/IP: Holding It All Together

So we have computers with open operating systems, networking tools to link them locally, and a worldwide telephone system to link them remotely. **But what holds it all together?** What is the digital glue that makes all this work in concert? A nifty set of rules known collectively as **TCP/IP**, that's what.

TCP/IP stands for Transmission Control Protocol/Internet Protocol. The word protocol is more commonly associated with diplomats and courtly schmoozing, and this is exactly why the word is so perfect for the Internet.

In the case of the Internet and TCP/IP, that objective is moving digital data from place to place, no matter where or how far apart those places are, no matter the quantity or the quality of the data. The collection of rules within the TCP/IP numbers around 100, and it can handle every aspect of data transport.

TCP/IP was originally developed to bridge satellite, radio and cable-based networks, and is a lowest common denominator protocol. An early networking project conducted at the University of Hawaii, dubbed the ALOHANet, needed to be linked to the ARPANet as part of the general effort to extend research activities through internetworking.

ALOHANet was a collection of computers linked with radios that broadcast data between themselves.

The effort to create a communications protocol between this network and the ARPANet led eventually and circuitously to TCP/IP.

TCP/IP is a digital passport that made possible open movement of files on the Internet, a bit like the difference between ordinary roads and tolls or private roads. TCP/IP is open to all travellers, and was ultimately selected as the official standard for the Internet in 1983.

TCP refers to the rules by which a message or file is broken up into 1500 character-sized datagrams or packets and transported. TCP controls how a piece of a message is addressed, the order in which the various bits of the message should be strung together at the other end, where the message came from, plus some error-checking and control information.

TCP breaks the data into 1500 character chunks because this is the maximum amount of data that IP can cope with at once.

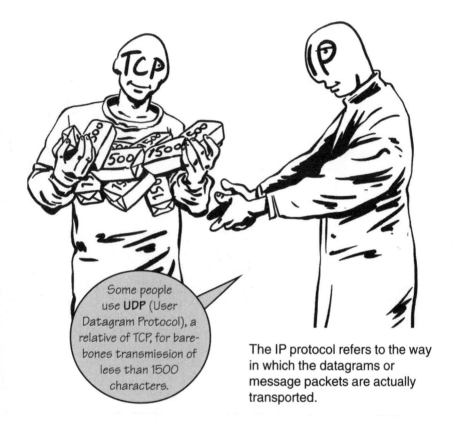

Some people use **UDP** (User Datagram Protocol), a relative of TCP, for bare-bones transmission of less than 1500 characters.

The IP protocol refers to the way in which the datagrams or message packets are actually transported.

IP gets the stuff to where it has to go, and TCP makes sure that all the pieces of the message arrive intact and that the entire messaging transaction is complete.

TCP/IP is an amazingly flexible set of rules, and although a few years ago the International Standards Organization decided on another standard for data transmission across disparate networks, virtually everyone on the Internet ignored them. Open Systems Interconnect (OSI) was invented by a committee in a laboratory and finally saw the light of day in 1988. With seven layers of protocols sitting one on top of the other, OSI lacks the organic beauty and perfection of something that has evolved through use, rather than something designed to serve a specific purpose. It is also a reminder that standards are not carved or drawn. They become apparent like the stranger in the mist who turns out to be your neighbour.

The implications of digital technology are more of a problem, though. Anything you do with a digital technology will leave automatically documented evidence for other people or computer systems to find.

These numerous developments were the seeds of the digital fabric now referred to as the Internet.

So we have telephone lines and computers working in tandem using TCP/IP. Advances in computing encouraged new approaches to how we worked with computer power, and computers soon evolved into shared systems whereby one powerful device managed the common activities of lots of less powerful desktop devices.

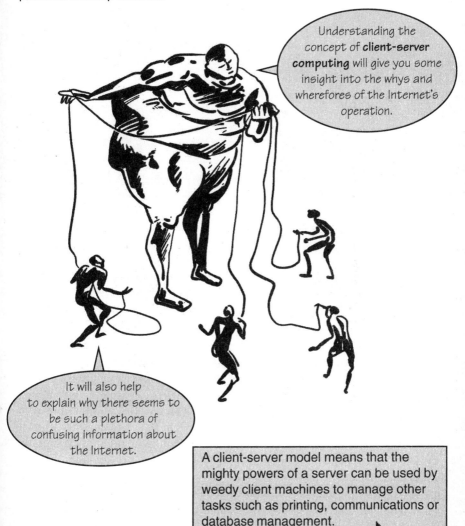

Understanding the concept of **client-server computing** will give you some insight into the whys and wherefores of the Internet's operation.

It will also help to explain why there seems to be such a plethora of confusing information about the Internet.

A client-server model means that the mighty powers of a server can be used by weedy client machines to manage other tasks such as printing, communications or database management.

All Internet services (and there are many) are based on client-server systems, but they don't necessarily all use the same rules for file access. Imagine a series of private fiefdoms that agree to work together using protocols that all of them support. On the Internet these various domains have their own ways of doing things, but they can all work together because of TCP/IP.

This is why you hear about ftp servers, Web servers, Gopher servers, Usenet servers, Telnet servers, WAIS (Wide Area Information Servers) and so on.
They all follow the general protocols of TCP/IP but have their own internal ways of doing things.

You can tell which particular fiefdom a server is part of from the resource descriptor in an Internet name, such as http, ftp, or Gopher. This defines the way different computers do what they do, and is the bit of the name which makes sure that host-to-host messaging happens without mistakes.

It's a bit like using money: everyone on the planet follows the same principles, but does not necessarily use the same currency. We have several ways to overcome these differences, including travellers' cheques and credit cards, the use of which is based on an agreed set of rules for monetary exchange.

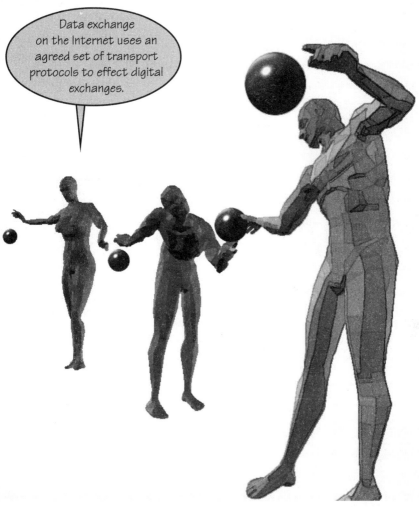

Data exchange on the Internet uses an agreed set of transport protocols to effect digital exchanges.

Networks of different kinds of servers used by clients with software suitable for that system exist all over the place. They connect over phone lines, and all support the TCP/IP set of rules for file transfers. Most of these digital hosts are publicly open to visiting guests, but there are some which choose to remain private, popularly known as Intranet sites.

Hackers take great delight in breaking into private Intranet sites (even on the Internet there are vandals), which are often protected by complicated software called **firewalls**. Access codes to exclusive private servers are encrypted, and hackers find it entertaining to break the encryption, leaving some footprint or trace of their presence, sometimes benign, sometimes not. Digital graffiti.

People like us are called crackers in the lingo.

We are like gate-crashers in the real world – the unwelcome guests that manage to get through the door, despite the efforts of the host to prevent us.

Unfortunately, vandalism on the Internet is not limited to gate-crashers. The Internet is a terrific way to distribute rogue software programs that have been written with the specific intention of causing damage. How much damage is subjective, but whether it's a trivial or traumatic matter, beware **viruses**. Worry about them, because although there's more fuss about viruses than there ought to be, they are very very annoying.

As the Internet grew, it soon became obvious that some sort of host-server naming convention would be necessary. Because there are so many computers in the world, many of them sharing resources over the Internet, naming is a very tricky problem. So to make life simple, there is now an agreed set of naming conventions used on the Internet: the Domain Naming System or DNS which is run by DNS Servers that convert the name you select into a set of numbers – the IP address that the Internet can use.

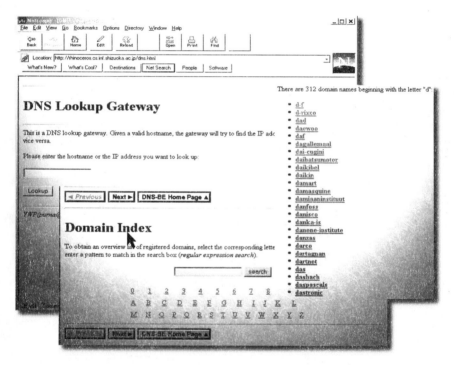

Two points about names: there are **names** on the Internet and there are **specified resources**. Uniform Resource Locators or URLs (formerly Universal Resource Locators) specify something such as a newsgroup or a file. On the Web, they act more like addresses in that they provide the destination of a hypertext link, a sort of road map. Don't worry about why there are two ways to express the same thing: a combination of semantic preference and history.

Remember, you can often learn more about a site from the things in front of the actual domain name. This information tells you what kind of site you are accessing. For example, http:// is the beginning of an address on the network of World Wide Web servers. You might also see ftp:// or Gopher://, which denote ftp or Gopher sites.

Like the World Wide Web, these types of sites are designed to improve search and retrieval of information, but they are older and less glamorous. They have been losing ground to the World Wide Web because of this, but they are nonetheless useful tools for storing and retrieving files. Ftp is still many people's preference for working with large files and software, because of its speed and the fact that it is a widely distributed resource.

For all Internet addresses there is a domain name, which is the bit that follows the @ symbol in an email address and refers to the server's name. This is followed by a top level domain code made up of a dot and a two- or three-letter code, often followed by a two-letter country code.

sean@sahara.co.uk

digitra@wastelands-unlimited.com

icon@mistral.co.uk

American domains don't have a country code after the domain name and top level domain, because until a few years ago country codes weren't really necessary.

Naming became problematic when the volume of users of the Internet reached a critical point, in much the same way as numbered street addresses became necessary as villages developed into towns.

There are nine top level domain codes which designate the type of host: **gov** means government, **int** means international organization, **net** means networking organization, **co** identifies a company or commercial enterprise, **com** is an American company, **mil** is military, **edu** or **ac** is an academic institution, **org** is a non-commercial organization of some sort.

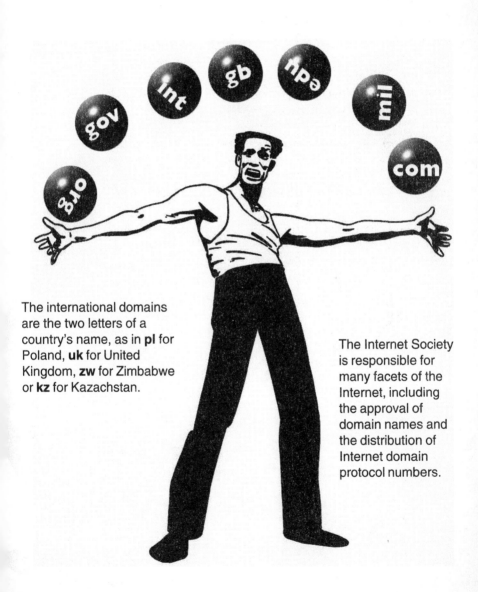

The international domains are the two letters of a country's name, as in **pl** for Poland, **uk** for United Kingdom, **zw** for Zimbabwe or **kz** for Kazachstan.

The Internet Society is responsible for many facets of the Internet, including the approval of domain names and the distribution of Internet domain protocol numbers.

An Internet domain protocol number or IP address is the number to which the domain name is mapped. The numerical equivalent of the letters in the name. Why bother, you may wonder? Well, this number is how the various computers operating across the Internet work out where to send files or messages that are moving from point to point across the network. It's meaningful to the IP bit of TCP/IP.

Clever stuff, and an integral part of the transport rules that get digital information from site to site.

Names can look as simple as this: **www.abc.com** or as horrid as this:

Besides domain names, there is the rest of the address. In an email, for example, the bit to the left of the @ sign is the user's name. The local computer handles the delivery of this part. The Internet itself handles the delivery of the message or file to the part of the address following the @. There can be all manner of other address detail on either side of the @, which is why some Internet addresses can look very long and complicated.

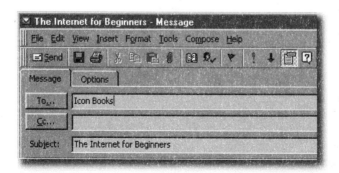

The address detail specifies the route within the computer that will lead directly to what you want to find. It's a bit like an indexing system at the library, with categories and subcategories, mirroring the directories and subdirectories on a large computer file system. This is why some addresses have this sort of thing:
ftp://pinky.perky.com/piggies/snouts/snuffle_snuffle_oink_oink/now

An analogue equivalent:

£ (you spend and earn pounds sterling) Peewee Jones (your name) @ the London Kingsley Hotel/the penthouse suite/the top floor/in room 99/ face down on the floor

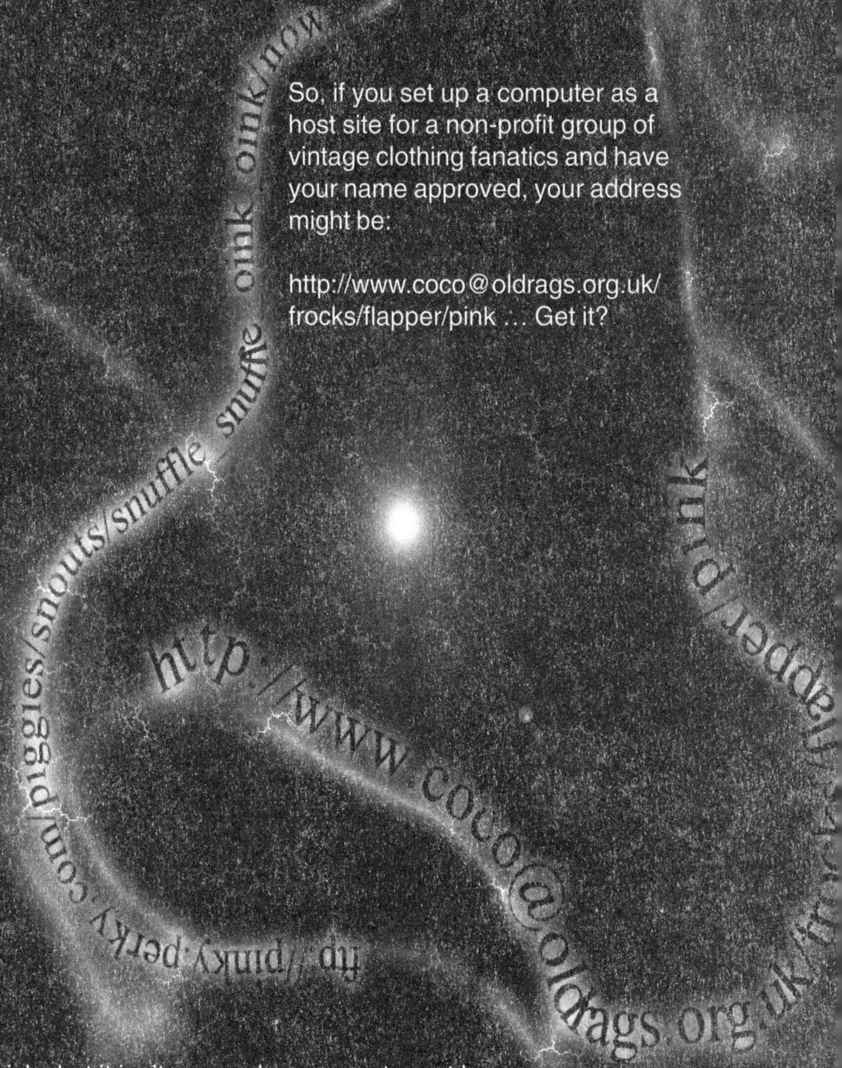

So, if you set up a computer as a host site for a non-profit group of vintage clothing fanatics and have your name approved, your address might be:

http://www.coco@oldrags.org.uk/ frocks/flapper/pink … Get it?

oink oink now

snuffle snuffle

piggies/snouts/snuffle

com/piggies/

ftp://pinky.perky.com

http://www.coco@oldrags.org.uk/frocks/flapper/pink

It looks tricky but it isn't, even when you get great long addresses. Most of the time you can get to where you want to go by using the main part of the address and then routing about on the server, once you are almost where you want to be.

Right, we've got a complex distributed system of computers that can communicate together over phone lines, using an agreed code of conduct. Together they create a vast repository of knowledge and information that anyone can access.

Why, then, isn't it simple?

Because it just isn't. The Internet can't be **simple**, although in practice it is easy.

The massive diversity of content and devices on the Internet has developed over time into a collective that works together. But you still need to appreciate some of the specifics of the Internet's components, to understand why there are so many ways to go wrong. For every service, for every computer, there are individual characteristics and quirks, just like people. This is why things are never simple.

The majority of Internet servers run one of two main multi-tasking operating systems, either a version of Unix (of which there are many, although all share common core operating functions) or Windows NT, invented by those lovely people at Microsoft. The NT stands for New Technology, a name so wonderfully imaginative that it's easy to understand what has kept the Mac community so loyal for so long to Apple. Servers run these operating systems, but desktop computers don't: they run Windows '95 or the Mac OS, or something else specific to a particular piece of hardware. This is because desktop devices don't need to perform as well or as cleverly as NT servers.

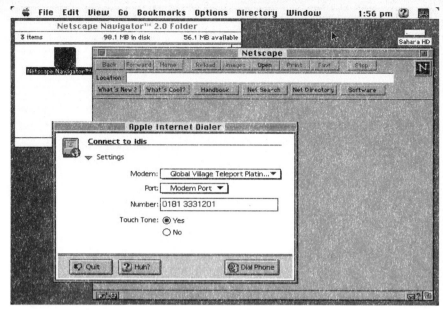

Mac OS

Win '95 / NT OS

43

Unix workstations are by far the most common form of host server on the Internet. Because Unix is **case sensitive**, treating upper case and lower case letters as different characters, this operating system is often responsible for weird errors. Never assume that just because your typing is letter perfect that you haven't made a mistake. Always check the case when specifying host file names.

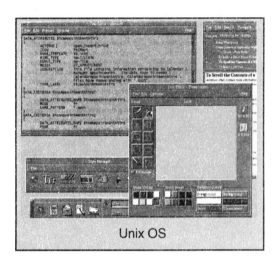

Unix OS

So what about host names? Well, everyone has a name and some means through which they can be reached, usually an address.

Computers are the same.

People give their computers names, ranging from "My Mac", or "Bibi's PC", just because it's more interesting than PC1, PC2, Mac HD99 or whatever.

In offices, you generally find people call their machines by user name and department, plus a number or some other naming convention or reference. If those computers are linked together on a local area network, the server in a client-server architecture uses the names to keep track of what's where and who's who.

Each user in such a set-up will have a private log-on to access the server, which is made up of a name and a password.

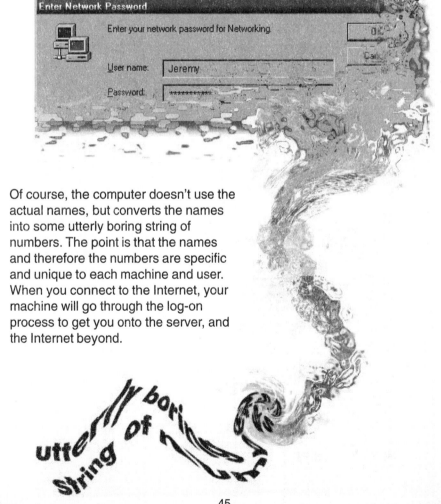

Of course, the computer doesn't use the actual names, but converts the names into some utterly boring string of numbers. The point is that the names and therefore the numbers are specific and unique to each machine and user. When you connect to the Internet, your machine will go through the log-on process to get you onto the server, and the Internet beyond.

The Internet is a homogeneous entity unified by a common acceptance of its rules and standards in communications protocols. **Modems** are a good example of how a common reason to cooperate can generate widespread and comprehensive standards.

It is populated by very clever people who understand its significance as a means of ensuring the continued forward movement of the human race. We must be confident that we won't let ourselves down.

"Modem" is a made-up word to abbreviate **modulator/ demodulator**. This device turns the digital data coming out of your computer into an analogue signal that can be transmitted over the telephone line. It will also translate an incoming analogue signal into digital information that is meaningful to your computer.

Modems let you know they are transmitting information by shrieking and whistling. They are vital for the Internet, although you won't need a modem if you have access to an ISDN line. The nifty modem/computer combos can also be used to send and receive faxes, as long as you have the necessary software.

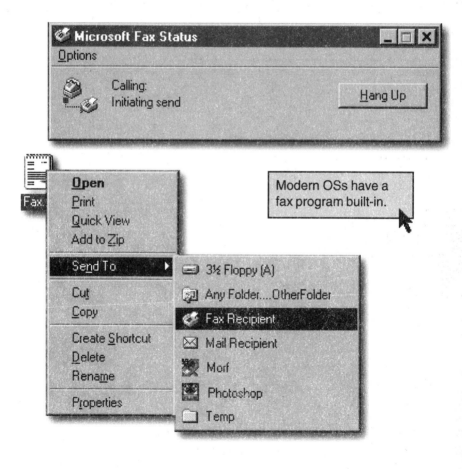

Modern OSs have a fax program built-in.

Modems are software-controlled, using SLIP or PPP. Serial Line Internet Protocol (SLIP) was invented so that IP packets could be transmitted over serial lines. The Point to Point Protocol (PPP) does the same thing, except that it supports asynchronous and synchronous systems, so it's more flexible.

There are all sorts of modems around, fitting into one of three main categories and classified according to how quickly they operate (their **bps** rate), how easily and helpfully they operate, and how much money they cost.

Remember, speed is everything on the Internet, so get the fastest modem possible.

The three modem types to consider are **internal**, **external** and **PCMCIA**, which is a removable one used in laptop computers.

Modems operate at varying speeds measured in bits per second (bps), ranging from 1200 bps which is slow to 33,600 bps which is alright. The slowest you should consider is 14,400 bps. There are problems going very much quicker than 28,800 bps on normal phone lines, because of the inability of the wires to twitter quickly enough beyond this speed. The maximum capacity for ordinary telephone lines is 54,000 bps.

Networking bods are predicting that ISDN (64,000 bps per channel and you can have lots of channels), switching technology to boost bandwidth, Gigabit Ethernet and ATM are the way of the future. ATM (Asynchronous Transfer Mode) transmits at various speeds, from 25 Mbps to 622 Mbps (that's **megabits** per second), and is being developed to handle 10 **gigabits** per second.

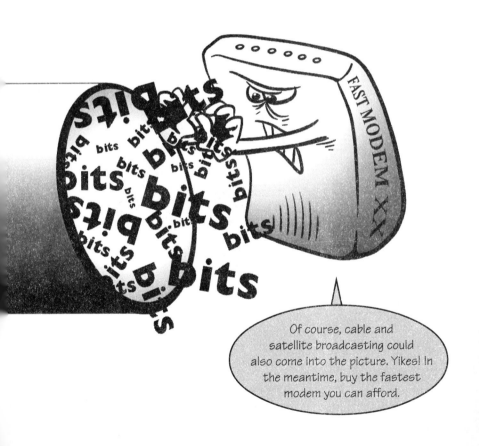

Of course, cable and satellite broadcasting could also come into the picture. Yikes! In the meantime, buy the fastest modem you can afford.

Modems can also do other things, such as check information coming in and going out for errors, compress information, automatically dial and answer the telephone, and tell you that they are doing something, useful or otherwise, by flashing little lights at you.

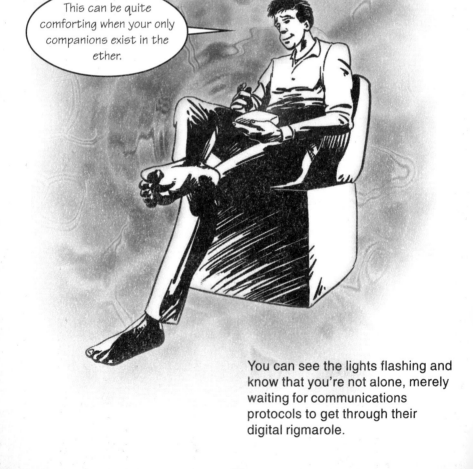

This can be quite comforting when your only companions exist in the ether.

You can see the lights flashing and know that you're not alone, merely waiting for communications protocols to get through their digital rigmarole.

You can tell that a modem does more than just squeal and flicker by the addition of either V22, V22 bis, V32, V32 bis, V42 or V42 bis to its name. These numbers refer to internationally recognized modem protocols that support various data rates, error correction between modems and data compression.

Error-checking modems can slow down data transfers.

Baud originally referred to the unit of telegraph signalling speed where one dot of Morse code per second was transmitted. **Émile Baudot** (1845-1903) invented the Baudot five-bit code system, along with the world's first teleprinter. Baudot code is still used on creaky telex machines, but its days are numbered. These days, Baud refers to a communication channel's capacity to carry information measured in terms of electrical oscillation.

Baud rate and bit rate are not the same, although they may be equivalent on slower speed modems.

Samuel Morse

Émile Baudot

Don't bother with the difference, just judge a modem by its bit rate, the number of bits per second. The higher the number of bits per second (bps), the better.

So the Internet is a collection of digital servers and client devices which function in a cooperative system using modems and ordinary telephone lines or dedicated digital phone lines such as ISDN.

The biggest problem with the Internet is that you still need a computer to use it. This, unfortunately, is something you must face, although one day your television will take care of this side of things. You will very likely be decaying by the time this actually happens, and unable to appreciate it. So sit down, look at the floor for a while, sigh a bit, ponder those days gone by when digital meant sticking your fingers up, and let it go. Computers are here to stay, and are part of everything (almost) that you do.

So what sort of computer should you think about for the Internet? Someone else's. This is the cheapest, easiest and most convenient type of computer to use on the Internet. It means you can avoid dealing with most of the boring details, and you can save on your telephone bill.

In fact, most Internet users have followed this method, accessing it from work or college. It is easily the best method to begin with.

If you haven't got a job, or an excuse to be at college, try your local library. Failing that, ask at your children's school, or make friends with someone nerdy enough to have a computer at home and be able to use it. This last is very important.

54

If the only way you can get onto the Internet is through your own efforts, you need to have some money or a credit card. Around £1,000 will do, although you will enjoy the Internet more if you are able to buy better equipment. You will need a computer and a modem.

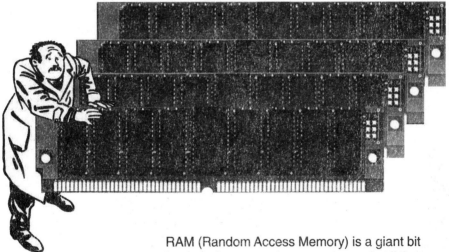

As far as the computer is concerned, buy as much processing power and RAM as possible.

RAM (Random Access Memory) is a giant bit bucket where your computer throws in all the bits it's working with (remember those binary digits) at a given moment, pulling out those it needs when it needs them. Imagine your clothes cupboard. Isn't it easier to find things when it isn't jammed full? RAM is like a cupboard. The bigger the RAM, the easier life is for your computer and for you.

When you are on the Web, you will be able to open multiple Web documents loaded with colourful exotic images and typography with ease, if you have 32MB RAM. If you have 16MB, life on the Internet will become very dull, depressing and monotonous. Get as much RAM as you can afford.

The bigger the better, because some data files (such as high resolution graphics) are very large. You may want to store lots of large files, and not having the room to do it is tedious. Think as well about the kind of operating system you want to work with.

Which Operating System?

An operating system (OS) controls the way the computer behaves. It is the thing that tells the machine what to do next when you turn it on. It controls the appearance of your screen, the access to disk drives, and so on. The operating system also controls the way in which files are stored on disk drives, and makes it possible for you to find what you are looking for. There are two main operating systems for desktop computers, the Mac OS and Windows '95.

There are others, but the Mac or a PC are probably a better bet because of the wealth of software development for these platforms.

Consider them both before you decide. Have a go on both PCs and Macs of various models at a local computer dealer until you have a preference. If neither suits, ask to test-drive an Atari or an Acorn, or a Silicon Graphics O2. Make sure you can get the applications needed to achieve what you want to do.

Application Softwares

Application softwares are computer programs that work beneath the operating system and do specific things. A computer and its operating system can run without applications, but applications cannot run without the operating system. Application softwares might do word-processing, accounting, drawing, page layout, image manipulation, send and receive electronic messages, or teach you to type. They depend on the operating system to control the computer and to ensure that everything they need to work, will work.

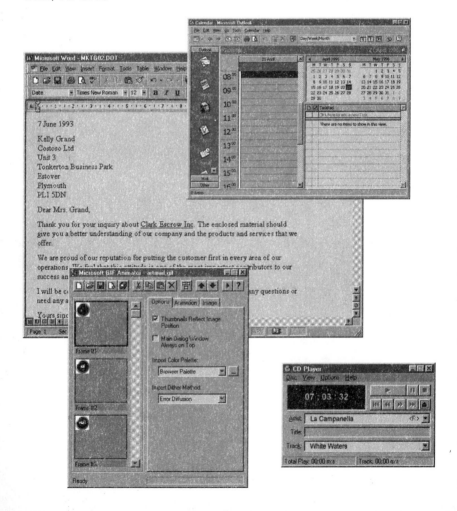

Make sure, if you buy additional software, that it's written for your computer's operating system. No point at all buying Word for Windows if you have a Mac. No point either in buying Photoshop 4.0 if you have an ageing Mac Classic. It won't work because the applications and operating systems are incompatible. It's a bit like buying a television in America and expecting it to work in Europe – or putting petrol in a diesel engine.

Computer Specs

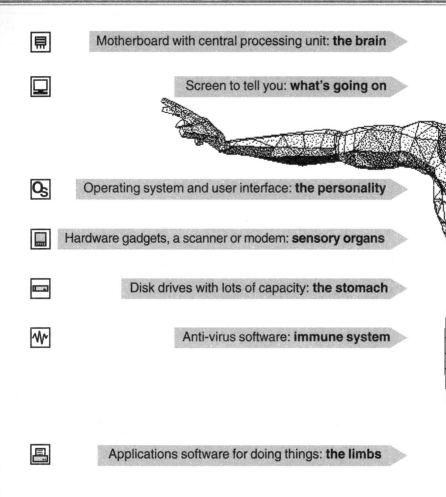

Motherboard with central processing unit: **the brain**

Screen to tell you: **what's going on**

Operating system and user interface: **the personality**

Hardware gadgets, a scanner or modem: **sensory organs**

Disk drives with lots of capacity: **the stomach**

Anti-virus software: **immune system**

Applications software for doing things: **the limbs**

So you've bought at least a Mac XXX or a PC XXX and a 33,600 bps modem. Make sure the computer's got all the necessary things to do what you want. If you want graphics on your computer, check that a good graphics card is included. If you want sound or multimedia, make sure you've got a sound card, speakers and a decent colour monitor showing millions of colours.

Recommended Minimum

Recommended minimum system for Mac OS: Power PC processor, 4 x speed CD ROM, 16MB RAM, 1MB video RAM, 14,400 modem, stereo sound, 1GB hard disk, colour monitor, keyboard and a mouse.

Recommended minimum system for Windows '95 OS: Pentium processor, 4 x speed CD ROM, 16MB RAM, 1MB graphic card, 14,400 modem, stereo sound card, 1GB hard disk, SVGA monitor, keyboard and a mouse.

Now you've got your computer and your modem and you've practised sending faxes and have some idea about how the software you've got works. You are reasonably comfortable with the idea of installing software (like parking a car, sometimes tricky until you get the hang of it). Make sure you are comfortable with your set-up, before you embark on the next stage.

Whatever machine you get, make sure you plan its set-up carefully and use common sense.

Make sure you understand what you've got and how it works, and that you can find your way about. Know as well where your computer will put the things you download from the Internet. And think about archiving and storage for all the wonderful things you will find. Be organized and tidy – or at least make a bit of an effort in the early stages to avoid confusion and frustration.

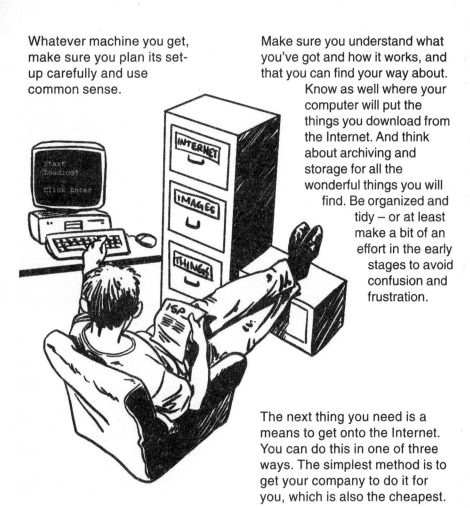

The next thing you need is a means to get onto the Internet. You can do this in one of three ways. The simplest method is to get your company to do it for you, which is also the cheapest.

Alternatively, you could lease your own incredibly fast and expensive ISDN line and be permanently connected to an Internet access node. You will not need a modem, but you will need an ISDN card added to the guts of your computer. Or you could use a modem to connect to an Internet Service Provider who owns access nodes. Whatever way you choose, you will have to pay for the access privilege.

The ISDN line is really only reasonable if you are providing access to a huge family, business, charity, etc., or if you expect to spend your life on the Internet!

Modem access is acceptable for most people, and it's the cheapest.

You ought to get all sorts of free software with your computer or your modem, or both. Amongst the muddle of programs, you will almost certainly find something to provide you with access to other computers. There may be a dedicated package, Eudora email for the PC and the Mac, for example. Both PCs running the Windows '95 operating system and PowerMacs running the Mac OS machines include TCP/IP software and email software.

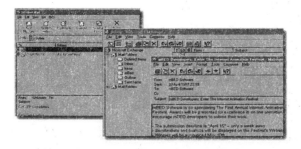

Internet access nodes are computers, mostly much more powerful than yours, that provide a common connection point between other parts of a local network and to other networks beyond. There are thousands of access nodes around the world, ranging from the humble to the megalofty. All support TCP/IP, that one vitally important technology that keeps the heart of the Internet beating, and binds together all aspects of computing and communications.

Internet access nodes differ in the number of accesses they can support at once, and how efficiently they can handle the incoming and outgoing traffic. The phrase "Point of Presence" or POP refers to a local computer owned and operated by an Internet Service Provider that you can dial **into** to get **onto** the Internet. It is one of those little phrases that you should try to understand, because it is part of the Internet lexicon, and you pay to use POPs.

Yes, I know ... They're getting more POPs every day ...

Don't pay for Internet access without questioning the service provider in great detail. Ask them lots of questions about what they do and how they do it. The most important question is how much they charge per month and whether they provide access at local call rates. There is no use working with an Internet Service Provider (ISP) who doesn't have lots of Points of Presence or an 0345 number.

Because if you live in the Orkneys and sign up with an ISP from Streatham with two POPs, your phone bill will be awful, and you'll get depressed because everything will be slow and dreary.

It is the Internet Service Provider (ISP) who charges you for accessing their POPs. An Internet Service Provider owns computers, modems, phone lines and employs people who understand computers. The ISP will provide you with a slice of time (generally on a monthly basis) to use these resources, along with a load of free set-up software; at least the good ones do.

In the same way as your membership to the leisure centre might give you access to several swimming pools, gyms and dance studios in your area, the ISP should be able to provide many points through which you can access the Internet.

As well as a lot of Points of Presence local to you, or accessible over an 0345 number, good service providers should provide a minimum of 28,800 bps access. They should have a good user-to-modem ratio. Eh? Your computer talks to the ISP's computer over the telephone line, each using a modem to pass messages between themselves.

A user-to-modem ratio of around 12:1 is about the minimum, otherwise you will spend your life gathering dust as you listen to a busy tone every time your modem dials the POP. This is another of the many reasons why people think the Internet is creaky and slow. Like so many other things in life, it isn't the technology, it's that there isn't **enough** of it.

The most important question to ask yourself, and answer before you start talking to service providers, is **what** you want to do, **how much time** you want to spend doing it, and of course **how often**. There is also the actual business of doing it to consider. How easily do you cope with DIY projects? How bothered are you about understanding the way things work? Do you want to spend hours and hours "configuring" (another word for the lexicon) your computer to talk to the service provider? How much free Web space will the ISP provide, and is this enough for your own site?

You have the choice, but you need to ask the service providers what you get for your money, and how much service they actually provide.

Configuring or setting up your TCP/IP software so that it knows about your computer, modem and ISP's telephone number is crucial to the success of your venture into the ether.

This set-up software is part of modern operating systems, but if you are likely to have difficulty with it, be sure that you work with an ISP who will help.

Still Waiting

If you have an Atari, an Amiga or an Acorn computer, the service could be very important. There isn't much in the way of Internet software for these machines, so some digital magic will need to happen on the service provider's server.

There are ordinary service providers and there are companies dedicated to providing their own private service, with access to the Internet thrown in. For international access, they are especially useful, because they have so many POPs. These providers have their origins as bulletin board services, and publish information themselves, saving you the editorial and access process. Bulletin boards have been around since the early days of computing.

They are like electronic cork boards on which members of a group can pin (or post) messages.

They were one of the early methods for exchanging information, and soon evolved into fully-fledged electronic mail systems as well as chat and news groups.

The best-known international services are CompuServe and AOL. There are other more localized services such as Microsoft Network (MSN), and those which are small and serve very specific communities of interest.

Each provides different benefits and has made different editorial decisions, particularly where **access to servers** on the Internet is concerned.

CompuServe hit the headlines in 1996 for their decision to bar access to certain lugubrious Internet offerings. They were accused of censorship, although they were exercising the editorial prerogative of a publisher.

With any service provider, there will be a monthly fee, and there may also be set-up fees. Find out what you get for your fee. Check that the time you get to use the Point of Presence isn't limited, either in terms of duration or access times. If you don't need the specific dedicated services of an online service such as CompuServe or AOL, choose an ISP which gives you unlimited net access at a flat monthly rate. Most ISPs offer this type of service.

A few service providers have cheap rate access, but if you don't plan to be up at 3:30 a.m. on alternate Wednesdays, it isn't really cheap.

You should also check out the support available. It is probably worth paying a set-up fee if you can be confident that you will never have problems getting on to the Internet thereafter.

There are all sorts of horror stories about Internet access, where users have spent up to a year trying to get predictable and reliable access. Sad really.

But the point is that letting the ISP handle your set-up ought to mean that your access is transparent and mindless.

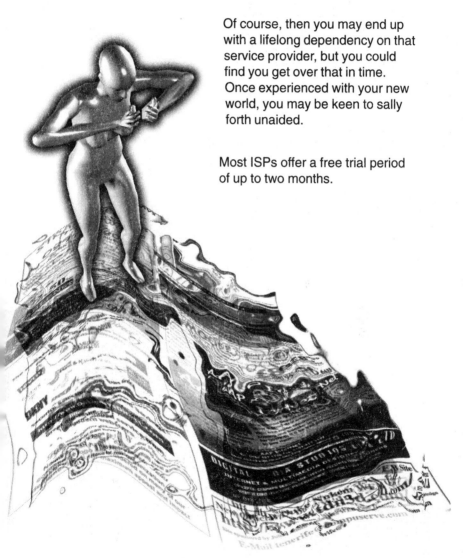

Of course, then you may end up with a lifelong dependency on that service provider, but you could find you get over that in time. Once experienced with your new world, you may be keen to sally forth unaided.

Most ISPs offer a free trial period of up to two months.

So now you know about the origins, purpose and method of the Internet. What next? The resources on the Internet, that's what. These are the many system-specific protocols that TCP/IP transports.

74

The ARPANet was never intended as a specific tool, but was set up as a utility. Once the developers were confident that it worked in principle, they started to use the network for other things, such as sending messages from point to point. This was the origin of electronic mail. The other thing they tried to do was to use computers as **terminal emulators** of some remote device.

After they figured out terminal emulation, the next step was to treat the connected computers as peers, actually passing digital files back and forth. Remember, they used different operating systems, so this was no trivial task. Thus was ftp born. But first Telnet, the next significant stratum of the Internet.

Telnet was designed for remote log-ins in 1969 and soon became popular as a means of resource sharing.

Apart from email, Telnet is the oldest service on the Internet. Today, Telnet is the protocol that allows you to log on to someone else's computer via the Internet, so you aren't paying the cost of a direct connection and are treated just like any other terminal user of that host machine. This is useful because if you're clever, you can use Telnet to bypass restricted sites, such as private newsgroups.

Telnet still uses a command line interface, however, and you will need to set up an account.

Telnet provides a bulletin-board-like interface for both public access and private systems.

Essentially, it is a layer between your computer and a remote system used to access and retrieve data indirectly.

These are generally very busy sites, and therefore you should expect very slow responses.

Telnet is used to launch external applications, as it is essentially a form of terminal emulation harking back to the days when users worked with dumb terminals that provided a view into the guts of a computer located elsewhere. If a password is required, using your electronic mail address often works. If it doesn't, you will need to get permission and a password. Once you are on a site you can use ftp to download and retrieve files.

You can now access Telnet sites through your Web browser.

Telnet is the usual mode for connecting to MultiUser Dimensions (MUDs). MUDs have their origins as adventure games and are mostly derivatives of *Dungeons and Dragons*. They are interactive. The idea of MUDs is to provide interactive fantasy worlds for several players. MUDs could also be useful for education and training, but they are not widely used for this yet.

Try http://medievia.netaxs.com:8080/ or newsgroup:rec.games.mud.diku

ftp predates the Web by many years
and is pretty much the original core of
the Internet. The first devices to
cooperate in a widespread
internetworked system used
a file transfer protocol to
ensure that files going from
one machine to another
arrived safely.

> ftp servers
> use an agreed **file transfer
> protocol** (or ftp), to make
> everything accessible to and
> from the outside world. Its
> origins are in the Unix world,
> so it is extremely
> powerful.

> But it can be
> tricky to work with,
> especially if you aren't
> particularly interested
> in struggling.

ftp is still the most widely used method for transferring large files across
the Internet, even though it gets the least populist attention. There is a
vast treasure trove of ftp sites with, among other things, all manner of
software utilities available for free or on a test basis (beware viruses and
bugs) and lots of shareware.

ftp sites are password-protected and require a log-in and password, but many are open and you can log on as an anonymous ftp user. By so doing, you can transfer or retrieve files, using your email address as a password. This last is a little Internet politeness, because most of the time it isn't necessary.

Universities, for example, will have a lot of traffic during the day and evening, but less in the middle of the night. If all you are doing is nosing about, do it when you won't get in someone's way.

You will need ftp client software. There are various programmes available, such as Fetch or Anarchie for the Mac, and WS-FTP or Cuteftp for Windows. The log-in procedures tend to vary with the package, so until you are sure you want to bother with direct access, start off exploring ftp sites via your Web browser.

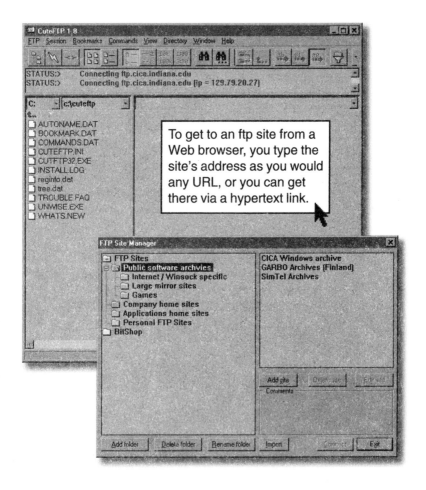

To get to an ftp site from a Web browser, you type the site's address as you would any URL, or you can get there via a hypertext link.

Follow the ftp site's log-on procedure and wait to be amazed and terrified when this appears on your screen …

You will be faced with an array of directories with thousands of files and will need to search through them to find what you want. A good start to an ftp session is getting any help files, index files, or things that look like site information. This will help you cut down file searching time and might prompt some other ideas for how to use the site's resources.

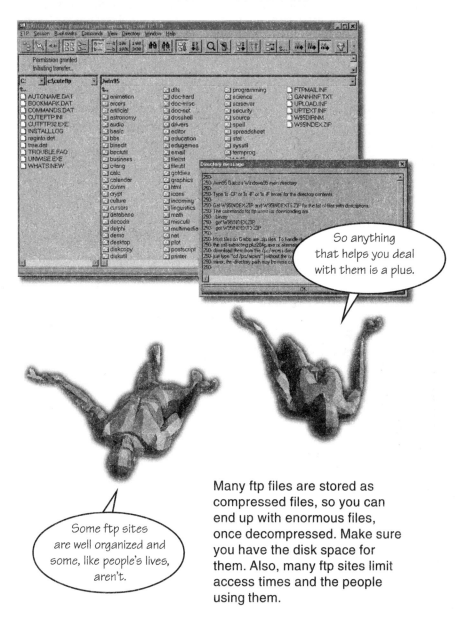

So anything that helps you deal with them is a plus.

Some ftp sites are well organized and some, like people's lives, aren't.

Many ftp files are stored as compressed files, so you can end up with enormous files, once decompressed. Make sure you have the disk space for them. Also, many ftp sites limit access times and the people using them.

You set up a session profile to instruct the program as to which ftp sites and directories you want to access. Basically, it's a form that the computer uses to make the connection.

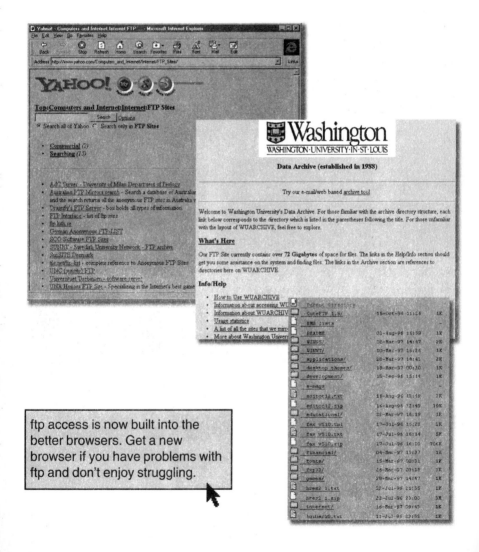

ftp access is now built into the better browsers. Get a new browser if you have problems with ftp and don't enjoy struggling.

You can also get to ftp sites via email, which is easy and you don't have to sit and wait. But you need to know ftp commands to instruct the server to conduct an anonymous ftp session. You send a message to
ftpmail@decwrl.dec.com
saying
subject: help
reply YOUR ADDRESS
connect THE SERVER ADDRESS OF WHERE YOU WANT TO GO
ascii SEND A TEXT FILE
chdir THE DIRECTORY YOU WANT
get THE FILE YOU WANT
quit END THE SESSION

One of the problems with getting onto ftp sites is knowing which ones you want to go to, and what they've got. Archie is used to locate ftp files, and is a system that indexes ftp sites, millions of them around the world. It is essentially the search engine for ftp sites, a computer program with a built-in ftp routine that has descriptive index searches for finding specific subjects and related subjects.

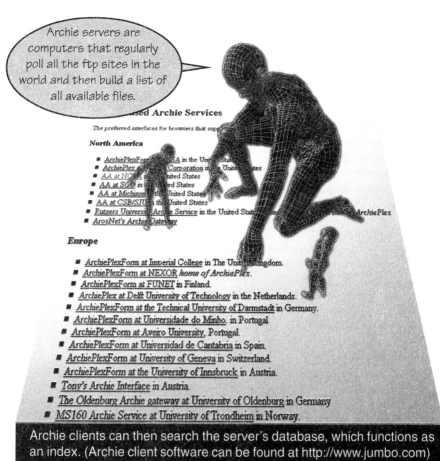

Archie servers are computers that regularly poll all the ftp sites in the world and then build a list of all available files.

...ed **Archie Services**

The preferred interfaces for browsers that supp...

North America

- ArchiePlexFo... ...A in the Un... Stat...
- ArchiePlex ... Corporation i... Unite... ...tes
- AA at NC... ...ited States
- AA at SC... in ...ed States
- AA at Michigan ...th...United State...
- AA at CSB/SJU... th... United States
- Rutgers Universi... Arc...e Service in the United Stat... ...ArchiePlex
- ArosNet's Archi...Gate...y

Europe

- ArchiePlexForm at Imperial College in The Uni... ...ngdom.
- ArchiePlexForm at NEXOR home of ArchiePlex.
- ArchiePlexForm at FUNET in Finland.
- ArchiePlex at Delft University of Technology in the Netherlands.
- ArchiePlexForm at the Technical University of Darmstadt in Germany.
- ArchiePlexForm at Universidade do Minho. in Portugal
- ArchiePlexForm at Aveiro University, Portugal
- ArchiePlexForm at Universidad de Cantabria in Spain.
- ArchiePlexForm at University of Geneva in Switzerland.
- ArchiePlexForm at the University of Innsbruck in Austria.
- Tony's Archie Interface in Austria.
- The Oldenburg Archie gateway at University of Oldenburg in Germany
- MS160 Archie Service at University of Trondheim in Norway.

Archie clients can then search the server's database, which functions as an index. (Archie client software can be found at http://www.jumbo.com) There are various servers running Archie, which means that although there ought not to be a difference, you should expect to look at several if you can't find what you want first time.

To get to an Archie server you need to type in the Unix command, use email, dedicated software, or go via your browser using a gateway to an Archie client. On the Web, Archie is slow but it presents its results as a Web page with a list of links to the various files it has found.

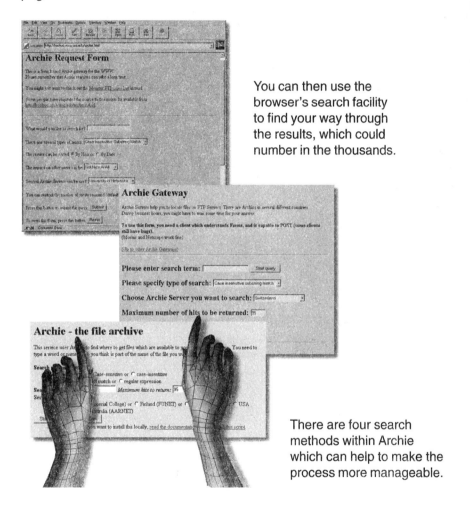

You can then use the browser's search facility to find your way through the results, which could number in the thousands.

There are four search methods within Archie which can help to make the process more manageable.

1. Exact match (exact) is what it says it is. **2.** Regular Expression Unix Match (regex) is horrid to use unless you speak Unix. **3.** Case Sensitive Substring Match (subcase). **4.** Case Insensitive Substring Match (sub). Subcase and sub are the most manageable. Sub is the slowest, but gives you the highest chance of finding what you want if you can't remember what it's called. You can also restrict searches to domain types, and to a limited number of types.

Send an email to archie@name of archive server, with
the word *servers* in the first line of the message body.
There are many Archie servers. Try archie.doc.ic.ac.uk
or archie.rutgers.edu to begin with.

North America

- ArchiePlexForm at NASA in the United States
- ArchiePlex at Amdahl Corporation in the United States
- AA at NCSA in the United States
- AA at SCO in the United States
- AA at Michigan in the United States
- AA at CSB/SJU in the United States
- Rutgers University Archie Service in the United States *based on an early ver*
- ArosNet's Archie Gateway

Europe

- ArchiePlexForm at Imperial College in The United Kingdom.
- ArchiePlexForm at NEXOR *home of ArchiePlex*.
- ArchiePlexForm at FUNET in Finland.
- ArchiePlex at Delft University of Technology in the Netherlands.
- ArchiePlexForm at the Technical University of Darmstadt in Germany.
- ArchiePlexForm at Universidade do Minho. in Portugal
- ArchiePlexForm at Aveiro University, Portugal.
- ArchiePlexForm at Universidad de Cantabria in Spain.
- ArchiePlexForm at University of Geneva in Switzerland.
- ArchiePlexForm at the University of Innsbruck in Austria.
- Tony's Archie Interface in Austria.
- The Oldenburg Archie gateway at University of Oldenburg in Germany
- MS160 Archie Service at University of Trondheim in Norway.
- Archie Service at University of Bergen in Norway.
- ArchiePlexForm at the Scientific and Technical Research Council of Turkey.
- ArchiePlexForm at LANET in Latvia.
- ArchiePlex at University of West Bohemia in Czech Republic.

You can use email to instruct Archie searches, which is a convenient and easy way to set them up to run offline.

Yes, gopher, but do you realize that we shouldn't appear until the next section?

Some email commands for Archie servers:
find
help
setsearch plus sub, subcase, regex, exact or leave blank to search with
default, so to sub site plus a host IP address or domain name to get list of
files on a particular ftp site.
quit
set mailto

The setsearch command tells Archie how to look for a match. The idea is
that the computer sifts through the digital deserts looking for the thing you
want. To help the process along you can give some additional instructions,
effectively programming the search process yourself. So type something
like this ...

setsearch sub, or

setsearch subcase

or setsearch regex

or setsearch exact

or merely setsearch

Once you've specified the search criteria you add to this slice of digital
exotica a well-rounded IP address or domain name, and Archie will
eventually present you with a rich and delicious list of files on the specified
site, that meet your needs. You can sit and wait patiently for the results, or
you can have them emailed to you using the following command at the end
of your message:

mail 100330.706@compuserve.com

for example.

Gopher is a more recently developed alternative to ftp for the transfer and archiving of files, a set of protocols that lies somewhere between the ftp server world and the Web world.

Gopher:

1. Various short tailed, burrowing mammals of the family Geomyidae, of North America.

2. Native or inhabitant of Minnesota: the Gopher State.

3. One who does errands or odd jobs.

4. Software that follows a simple protocol for searching through internet, and retrieving docu

The idea with Gopher was to come up with a navigation system that would make it easier to work with directories and file lists.

Gopher uses a menu-based hierarchical system of document retrieval. Gopher is much easier than working with Archie and ftp, because of its more user-friendly file structure and built-in search mechanisms. Gopher sessions invariably work, which isn't always the case with ftp.

The only big problem with Gopher is that it is slow, and it requires site administrators to create the Gopher menus in the first place. There are faster ways to pootle about in ftp land.

Indeed, ftp is still the most popular file transfer method on the Internet.

Use Fetch or Anarchie for the Mac or Cuteftp for Windows. Because the Web recognizes Gopher and ftp protocols, you can also access these sites from your Web browser, and you can add Web bookmarks to GopherSpace, as it's called.

By the time you read this, it will very likely be possible to upload files to ftp sites from the World Wide Web. With every week that passes, the Web becomes ever more the easy window onto the Internet at large.

You can find out what is on Gopher sites by using Very Easy Rodent Orientated Netwide Index to Computerized Archives, or Veronica, a relative of Archie. Veronica looks through the network of Gopher sites for what you have specified in your search request.

There is also an index routine to help you find your way around the server you are on.

Jonzy's Universal Gopher Hierarchy Excavation and Display, or Jughead, works like Veronica but only searches local directory names, so it's quicker. Not all Gopher sites support Jughead, but all support Veronica. Both programs work in the same way, but have a few differences in commands and functionality.

One of the earliest uses for the Internet was email, an asynchronous form of electronic communications (you can't send and receive data at the same time).

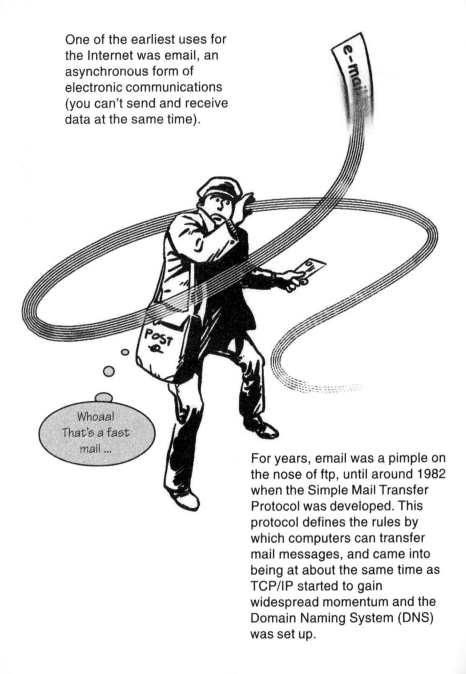

Whoaa! That's a fast mail ...

For years, email was a pimple on the nose of ftp, until around 1982 when the Simple Mail Transfer Protocol was developed. This protocol defines the rules by which computers can transfer mail messages, and came into being at about the same time as TCP/IP started to gain widespread momentum and the Domain Naming System (DNS) was set up.

So you send messages to
someone and wait for a reply.
It looks like this:

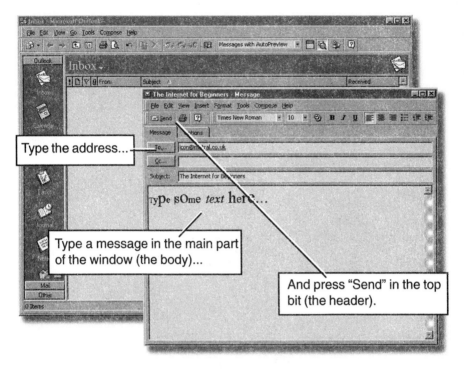

Type the address...

тyPe ѕОme *text* her℮...

Type a message in the main part
of the window (the body)...

And press "Send" in the top
bit (the header).

Your computer sends it to a service provider.
The service provider's computer sends it out
over the Internet, which makes sure it
reaches its destination.

It's like the phone system, but with a major
difference. When you dial a telephone
number, the switching circuitry locates the
number and opens a channel. The person at
the other end answers, and bingo! you have
a dedicated communications channel just for
you and your friend. But no one else can
share it (unless something goes wrong) and
that's why the Internet will replace the phone
system one day: it opens a channel with
multiple points of access.

There are loads of free and shareware email programs around, such as Pegasus for the PC or Eudora for Mac and PC. There are many features that you will need, or not, depending on what you want to do. It's a bit like choosing a telephone.

Do you want to store loads of numbers, view them, annotate them, have the phone prompt you to change them, and so on?

In software, as in anything else people do, you can find a package to suit your needs. Start off simply and get comfortable with the medium before you try to do anything clever, though.

Hmmm ... this might be a bit big for me ...

There are all sorts of conventions and rules that users of email and the Internet in general ought to follow. Lamentably referred to as Netiquette (at least it isn't another acronym), this is essentially a code of behaviour for the dispossessed of the ether. There are basic courtesies, such as brevity and directness, using polite language, and so on.

There are conventions, such as not using capital letters unless you want to express shouting LIKE THIS. There are quite dreadful manipulations of the limited ASCII character set used to convey all sorts of emotions and responses (ASCII doesn't include many symbols or accented characters which is why some things appear garbled on emails):

:-) HAPPY   :-(SAD   :-o SURPRISE

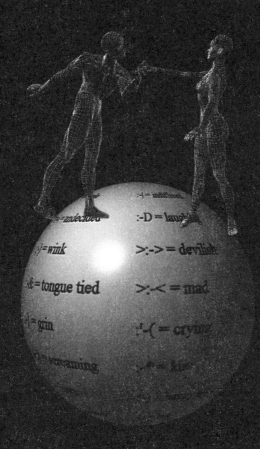

:-| = indifferent
:-D = laugh
;-) = wink
>:-> = devilish
:-& = tongue tied
>:-< = mad
:-| = grin
:'-(= crying
:-O = screaming
:-* = kiss
= undecided

Pathetic really. These are called **emoticons** and they are best left to the <=:-) (dickheads) who enjoy them so much. There are also little abbreviations that people like to use, such as IMHO (in my humble opinion), RTFM (read the fucking manual) and ROTFL or rolling on the floor laughing. The latter can save time and be useful, but as to the former, LITTW (leave it to the wankers).

Guidelines for online behaviour are just that – they are not supposed to be prescriptive.

A word of warning. Don't ever dash off messages thoughtlessly.

Write emails offline so that you can be sure you say what you mean, mean what you say, and can do what you say you will do. Consider what you write and don't forget the import and interpretation of words.
This will also help to keep the phone bill down.

Many people think that email has revived the art of letter writing. Pah! Once you get the hang of it and the novelty's worn off, you will be just as disinclined to write to people as you were before.

There are several data-encoding standards used in email. They provide a means of converting binary codes which are unreadable into ASCII characters which are. As in …

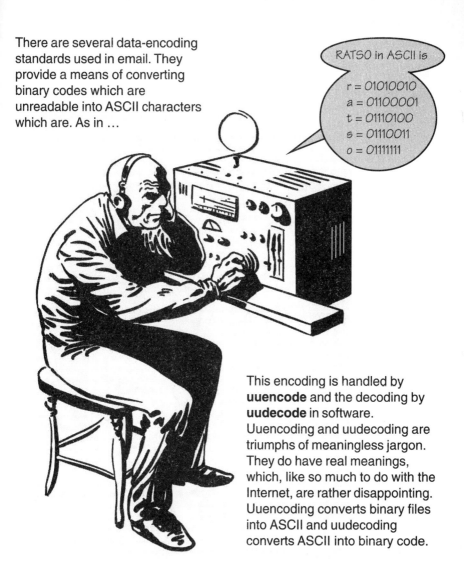

RATSO in ASCII is

r = 01010010
a = 01100001
t = 01110100
s = 01110011
o = 01111111

This encoding is handled by **uuencode** and the decoding by **uudecode** in software. Uuencoding and uudecoding are triumphs of meaningless jargon. They do have real meanings, which, like so much to do with the Internet, are rather disappointing. Uuencoding converts binary files into ASCII and uudecoding converts ASCII into binary code.

Look on ftp sites for more about this if it matters to you, which it should. Encoding and decoding techniques never seem to work the same way twice. Don't be surprised or disheartened if you have problems. It's just a phase.

Multipurpose Internet Mail Extensions or MIME is a standard for non-text files, used to attach images or multimedia files to emails. The problem with MIME is that both ends of the email, i.e. sending and receiving, have to be MIME-compliant. Often they aren't, which is why MIME attachments don't always come through.

You can tell how a file is encoded by its three-letter suffix:

.hqx is a BinHex encoded file (BinHex is a Mac-only encoding system that also requires both ends to be the same. In this case, they must both be Macs. BinHex turns binary files into ASCII)
.JPG or **jpeg** is JPEG compressed graphic
.BMP or **.PCX** bitmap graphics
.AVI video for Windows
.MID for midi files
.WAV for Windows sound files
.AIFF for Mac sound files
.PDF the portable document format
.PS a PostScript file
.TXT for text
.SGML for SGML documents

There are many of these and the list is growing all the time ...

Remember, file types and extensions are good ways of working out what something is.

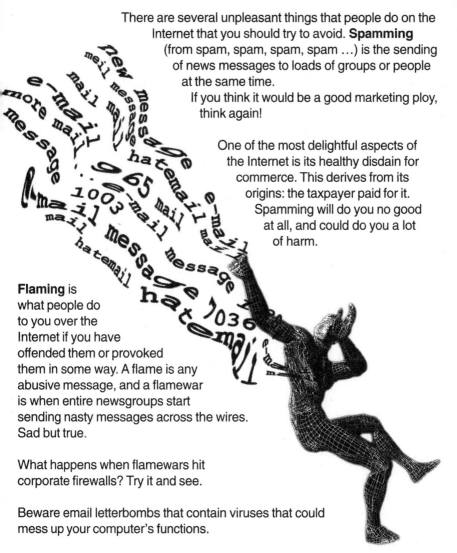

There are several unpleasant things that people do on the Internet that you should try to avoid. **Spamming** (from spam, spam, spam, spam …) is the sending of news messages to loads of groups or people at the same time.

If you think it would be a good marketing ploy, think again!

One of the most delightful aspects of the Internet is its healthy disdain for commerce. This derives from its origins: the taxpayer paid for it. Spamming will do you no good at all, and could do you a lot of harm.

Flaming is what people do to you over the Internet if you have offended them or provoked them in some way. A flame is any abusive message, and a flamewar is when entire newsgroups start sending nasty messages across the wires. Sad but true.

What happens when flamewars hit corporate firewalls? Try it and see.

Beware email letterbombs that contain viruses that could mess up your computer's functions.

Also beware mailbombs, whereby some person of limited imagination sends a huge number of emails to someone, in the hope that the volume of data will crash their machine.

Mailing lists are subscriber-supported discussion groups which evolved in the early days of the Internet. Because they work with email software, there is no special routine to go through, as there is with newsgroups. Mailing groups' email addresses are located all over the Internet, on ftp, Gopher, WWW and other sites.

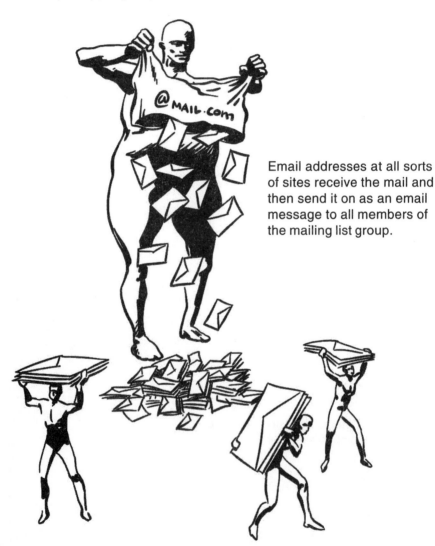

Email addresses at all sorts of sites receive the mail and then send it on as an email message to all members of the mailing list group.

For every mailing list, you have two addresses: the mailing address which uses a mail reflector to forward mail to sets of other addresses (i.e. to the people on the list), and the administrative address. This handles the general management and maintenance of the list. As with newsgroups, there is no single list or central directory of what's out there, so you just have to plunge in. Try bit.listserv.new-list for an idea of what's out there.

This is a list of mailing lists people have compiled. Although cumbersome to use, it will give you some idea of where to start.

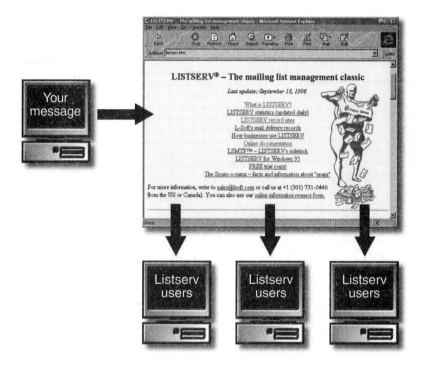

You can set up a mailing list of your own, and you can turn your mailing list into a newsgroup if you can get it sanctioned by news.group. This

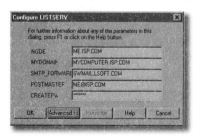

isn't necessary with alt (alternative) groups, which is why the weird and wonderful reside there.

Contact
listserv@bitnic.educom.edu or
news.newusers.questions\
for more information.

These days there are two major automatic mailing list managers or programs, ListServ and MajorDomo. The largest category of mailing lists is the ListServ type.

ListServ is a computer program that was originally developed to manage mail on BITNet (Because It's Time Network). Now the vast majority of ListServ mailing lists reside on the Internet, and there are only a few thousand BITNet-based ListServ groups. These servers also carry other non-ListServ administered mailing lists, such as MajorDomo which is the same as ListServ, except it uses different commands. Both are basically mail server software programs.

ListServ automates the administrative side of mailing lists using electronic mail requests. Users send a series of commands as an email to a ListServ server to be added or removed from mailing lists. ListServ can also retrieve files from remote archives. There are some moderated ListServ groups, called peered ListServ groups, where messages are monitored and checked.

ListServ sites can handle thousands of different mailing lists, serving thousands of communities of interest from blackjack players to bromiliad growers.

ListServ addresses are made up of the group name, the ListServ site, possibly followed by .BITNet.

In both cases, make sure you don't confuse messages with instructions to the server. They aren't the same, because people read and respond to **messages**, but computers read and respond to **instructions**.

Mailing lists can't keep track of message sequences. Nor do they post messages in a sensible order. This can make conversations a bit hard to follow. These mailing lists can generate an enormous amount of data, which usually arrives in a mess of files muddled in with your ordinary emails. To make the information more manageable, many people use the Message Digest command to get a single consolidated file with all the messages posted in a day. You can turn this on and off at will.

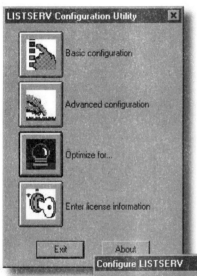

You can also instruct a ListServ or MajorDomo site to manage your messages. The program can be set up to give you an acknowledgement when you send a message, or to provide information about group members, or to keep secret information about you, or to stop sending messages on a specific topic or during a certain period of time, such as when you are on holiday.

It is also possible to administer mailing lists manually. Many discussion groups are managed in this way. You get onto manual lists in the same way as you get onto automated ones, by sending an email to the administrator. The difference is that you are communicating with a sentient being, so you can use natural language instead of program commands. Mailing lists can also be overseen by a moderator who can choose to delete messages deemed inappropriate. Nannies.

Welcome to the ND HECN LISTSERV Server
North Dakota Higher Education Computer N   04/09/97
  LISTSERV.NODAK.EDU Public Files

Up to higher level directory
  LISTSOF.LISTS   Wed S
  NEW-LIST.CATALOG   bytes Wed
  NEW-LIST.CREATE   2 Kb
  NEW-LIST.DBINDEX   539
  NEW-LIST.DBNAMES
  NEW-LIST.DBRINDF   840 Kb   T
  NEW-LIST.DIGEST   33 Kb   Fri May
  NEW-LIST.DISCLAIM   536 bytes Wed May
  NEW-LIST.FORMAT   9 Kb   Fri Mar
  NEW-LIST.LOG8901   43 Kb   Wed May
  NEW-LIST.LOG8902   23 Kb   Wed May
  NEW-LIST.LOG8903   19

Your first request to any list, once you're on, should be for information on how to work with the list.

Although most mailing lists are public, there are some private ones that you can only join by invitation. Mailing lists are related to newsgroups in that they are forums for special interest discussions, but they differ in the way in which messages are distributed. Mailing lists use email, whereas newsgroups use dedicated software.

A newsgroup is a more sophisticated version of a mailing list where messaging is more like a series of dialogues. You need newsreader software to make it work.

> Another good thing to ask your ISP is how many newsgroups they can access.

There are thousands and thousands of newsgroups on the Internet. If you happen to know one that you want to access, impress the service provider by asking to get access to it. If they can't, they soon will if they want your business.

So what's a newsgroup? It's a special interest group, a sort of digital grapevine cum gossip forum within the UseNet community that use the Network News Transfer Protocol, another of those Internet domains. These groups pass messages to group members and are set up by individuals who have some issue to raise or some particular interest to share – a bit like mailing lists which forward email to a special interest group.

They can be either free-form meaningless sessions or they can be moderated.

Moderated newsgroups tend to stay on track a bit better than the unmoderated ones, but the moderator can exercise control over the discussions. To participate in a newsgroup, you need to subscribe (and unsubscribe when you've had enough). It isn't likely you will be asked to pay, except for some of the more élitist groups. In the language of the newsgroup nerds, if you browse through newsgroups but never actually subscribe to them, you are being a **lurker**.

Newsgroups are a means of newsgathering. They support "conversations" in the form of message threading. The responses to messages are posted in sequence, so you can follow a line of discussion. Messages are held on the server as long as there is space for them, and that will be governed by how much traffic there is on the server, and by how much disk storage a server has provided for newsgroup messages.

You can access newsgroups either via a browser or using a dedicated newsreader program. The newsreader program will have more features, but just **what** will depend on the service provider's news server.

Ask them if they can give you full access to UseNet. UseNet can work without an Internet connection, since it uses its own protocols.

As long as you can connect to a local area network which can access other UseNet sites, you're on the UseNet network. Fortunately, these sites also use TCP/IP, which is why they are available to the entire Internet community.

UseNet is second only to email in terms of its usefulness and popularity. There are several major UseNet categories: **soc** for social issues, **sci** for science, **talk** for debate, **rec** for leisure and hobbies, **comp** for computer stuff, **news** (the best place for beginners), and **misc** for anything else. There are other **alt** (alternative) categories and **sig** (special interest) categories for things not covered in the main set, usually of limited appeal.

To participate in a newsgroup you will need newsreader software. Most online services have their own newsreaders, so there isn't any need to bother with set-up if you get onto the Internet via an online service provider. Most ISPs provide this as part of their service, but you should ask, and if they don't, be prepared to do it yourself. It isn't hard, just boring. You should get a copy of Gravity, WinVN or OUI if you have a PC, or Nuntius or Newswatcher if you have a Mac.

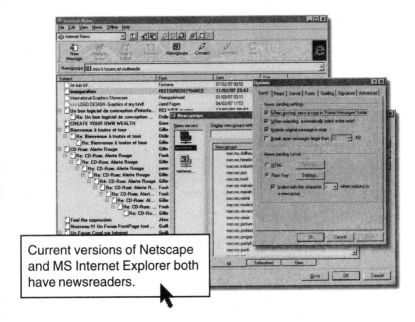

Current versions of Netscape and MS Internet Explorer both have newsreaders.

Set-up involves accessing the news server, details of which you should get from your ISP.

If you want to subscribe to a group that isn't on your ISP's list, you will need to get the ISP to subscribe and make the newsgroup available to its members. There are some 18,000 newsgroups, many of which will not be available to you through your ISP because they are of marginal interest or are dedicated to interests that the ISP decides should not be encouraged. You should probably trust your ISP on this, but if you really want to be convinced, find the address yourself and go direct to the site using Telnet.

Once you have selected and subscribed to the groups of your choice, you can instruct your newsreader to display only these. This is preferable to having the server's 12,000-odd appear every time you open the application.

Messages are marked by the newsreader software as read when they are opened.

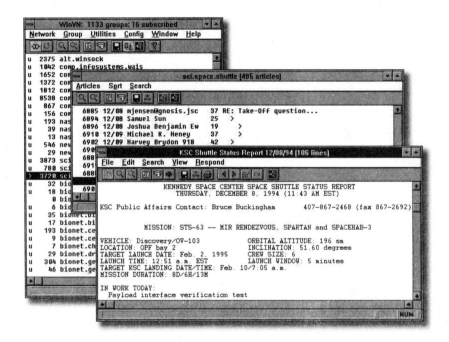

You can also mark messages yourself as read, even if you haven't, to prevent them coming back – one way of ignoring boring communicants. This way you only see new messages and can more closely define a discussion group if you want. Alternatively, you can save messages that you want to keep, or mark as unread (even though you've read them) those you want to keep seeing. This will only work for as long as the message is on the server, though. Eventually it will disappear into the digital ooze.

You can also cut and paste what you find into other applications, search through it, send it elsewhere, respond to it privately or whatever, using email.

ROT13 has become a useful convention for warning you that a newsgroup contains discussions that are likely to offend you. ROT13 is a substitution cypher, a simple encryption code whereby characters are replaced by the letter that occurs thirteen places ahead in the alphabet. Newsreaders mostly have the command to unscramble the cypher.

Messages, referred to as **articles**, are made up of the **message body** (which you care about) and the **header** (which the computer cares about). This, as with email, is where the information about the sender's address and the subject are contained.

Newsgroup messages are called articles because participants fancy themselves the next generation of information broadcasters.

And they may be right!

Remember, newsreaders can only cope with ASCII characters, and automate the attaching of MIME or uuencoded files to include binary data converting .GIF, .JPEG, .BMP and formatted files to their original format. If your newsreader doesn't do this automatically, find newsreader software that does.

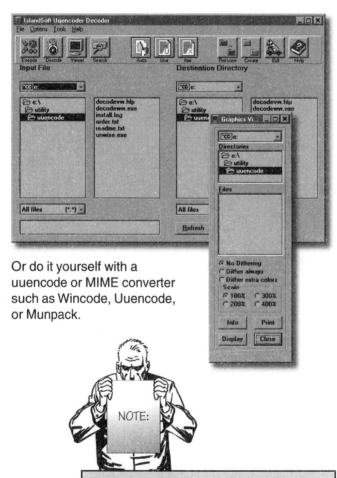

Or do it yourself with a uuencode or MIME converter such as Wincode, Uuencode, or Munpack.

NOTE:

There is no ASCII character for pounds sterling, so use words when talking about sterling currency.

You can also log onto news servers other than your own ISP's. Some have restricted access, but others welcome the public at large. These are likely to be busy, but if you can't find the group you're looking for on your own server, look elsewhere.

Beware the addictiveness of newsgroups. It is easy to get caught up in endless philosophizing and pointless pontifications. This is expensive in terms of your phone bill and time.

The Web is fast becoming the most popular tool for finding things on the Internet, and is certainly the most hyped. The boundaries between the Web and other parts of the Internet are now blurred, largely because the Web supports a wide range of protocols. It automates all the dreary bits, but because it is processing all those automated instructions it is much slower than ftp.

The Web is not necessarily the most widely used, despite the hype.

One of the reasons for the Web's popularity is that it is a **graphical system** which combines words, typography and images on screen.

Pictures and a simple but well-designed page of text are indeed much easier to deal with than things like this.

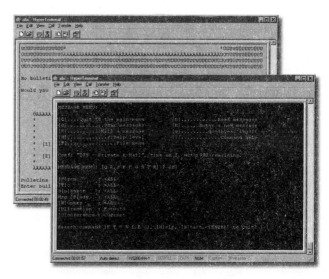

Plus you can design your own site, presenting a very specific image to the world beyond, using words, pictures and sound.

Therefore the WWW has a much wider-ranging power to communicate. The Web reaches out to people who are probably familiar with a desktop computer's graphical user interface, but are unlikely to have the foggiest idea about log-ons, passwords and other such digital choreography.

Browsers such as Netscape Navigator and Microsoft's Internet Explorer automate the search, access and retrieval of files, so that the whole process is nearly mindless.

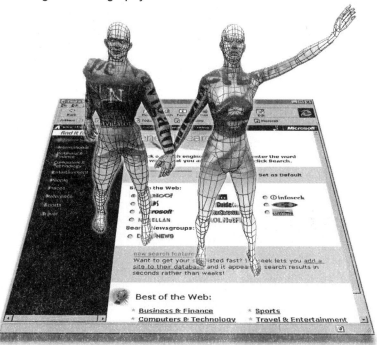

Users do not need to know or understand the underlying technology responsible for the automation, which makes the Web very compelling.

The Internet reaches beyond geographic, social and political boundaries, and the Web takes it over the linguistic one as well, at least in terms of computer languages.

Web servers all use the **hypertext transfer protocol** (http) to send hypertext information out over the Internet. The use of a common protocol has, as with ftp, Telnet and so on, created yet another community within the Internet. However, the Web is unique because of its flexibility and its ease of use. Together, the WWW and HTML provide graphical hypertext-linked access for less computer-literate users. The Web is fast becoming a superset of all other Internet activities.

The **HyperText Markup Language** or HTML provides the building blocks for documents on the Web. The term **hypertext** was coined in 1967 by Ted Nelson at MIT, to express the idea of a collection of documents with automatic cross links so that you could read a random selection of information. Hypertext has some fascinating implications, because it can be used to create derivative documents from random selection of material.

People will be able very easily to create books which are dedicated to specific areas of interest by gathering the content themselves from publicly available documents.

Ted Nelson

In 1989 Tim Berners-Lee, working at the CERN Laboratories in Switzerland, defined the http protocol that made it possible to link documents across servers. He developed a network of links using hypertext to create a web of documents located at numerous research sites. The protocol worked alongside the many other Internet-based protocols.

But it wasn't until the development of Mosaic in 1993 that the Web as we know it today started to evolve as a specific part of the Internet.

Tim Berners-Lee

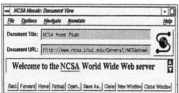

Mosaic is a viewing/browsing technology developed by a couple of students at the University of Illinois to create a graphical layer that would sit on top of the Web, making content retrieval more user-friendly, and the Web easier to use.

HTML or the HyperText Markup Language is an SGML (Standardized General Markup Language) Document Type Definition (DTD) that defines the format of a document. But its appearance will depend on how a given viewer or browser decides to interpret those format commands or HTML tags. Tags are like typesetters' marks that identify what's what on the page. Look at a newspaper story or a page in a book. There will be headlines, bylines, chapter heads, page numbers, various paragraphs and so on. These all look different because they have been designed specifically to make the content easy to read.

Hypertext and HTML let you leap from page to page, page to site, or indeed anywhere, because the technology can link content.

A bit like the way encyclopedias contain page references to items of interest in other volumes, except with hypertext and HTML the computer does the finding and opening for you. That's what hypertext is – **digital content awareness** that provides a digital equivalent to your ability to remember things and find them.

The HTML standard and the various things you can do with it is the subject of much bickering. On the one hand, the World Wide Web Committee responsible for its development doesn't get new features into the language quickly enough. On the other hand, the commercial browser people add HTML features that work best on their browser and not all that well on their competitors' products. The new commands are not exactly standards, so people get a bit worked up about it.

World Wide Web Committee

It's ultimately down to the World Wide Web Committee to pull their finger out, or provide a means of validating new additions to HTML or of notifying Internet users of their shortcomings.

HTML only works with ASCII text, so remember always to save your words as straight text (with the .txt extension, and specify in the Save command that the file format is text only). Saving things as straight text removes all the cosmetic glitz such as type styles and design layout, and leaves only the unformatted text.

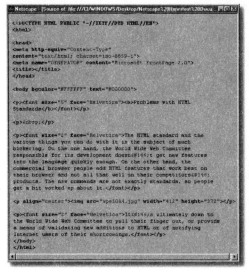

Previous page in HTML code ...

... and as it would look in a browser

"<" and ">" always appear in pairs and are a signal on the Web that something is a special code and that it contains special instructions for the browser. The browser then follows the instructions and formats the raw ASCII data into something more presentable on the screen. The details of the instructions are hidden behind the codes and you will only see, for example ... <TITLE XXX> but the browser will render it XXX.

Instruction tags are generally in pairs, but not always. For instance, <P> tells the browser to end one paragraph, throw in a blank line, and start another paragraph. Use it if you want to add lots of space between paragraphs, as without it all carriage returns and spaces get collapsed into one. Or use <BR> to create a single line break.

Anchor tags create links from one document to another, and are made up of the link tag which is the HTML tag that says "this bit is an address you need to leap to" and the URL for the destination of where to leap. So there are two things that happen when the browser encounters an anchor tag: the browser is told "time to go" and then sees where to go to. This is the identifying information: <A> HREF=http://www.sahara.co.uk </A>

The Web has become a superset of the Internet, able to handle its own protocols plus numerous others. Browsers can now recognize resource descriptors from URLs, and the power of search engines to reach across the Internet is extending all the time.
Browsers are also a good way to organize your space and will get increasingly integrated with the desktop, so that using the Internet will be just like using any other resource on your computer.

You are a browser and you use your brain to find your way through life, remembering things as long as you can, taking note of the things that interest you and that you want to pursue.

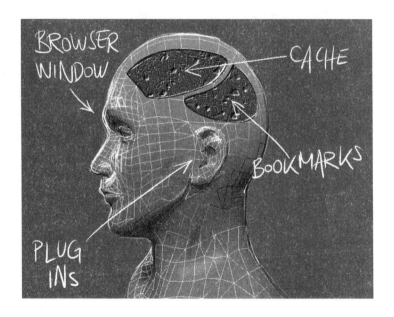

... **cache memory** is where what you've been thinking about and doing lately stays until something more current takes its place.

... **bookmarks** (in Netscape Navigator) or **favourites** (in Internet Explorer) are the digital equivalents of mental notes, reminders to yourself of somewhere you want to return to.

Browser technology is evolving quickly and becoming increasingly modular, so you can configure your browser to suit your way of working. This could be very simple or extremely complex.

The two most popular browsers are Netscape's Navigator and Microsoft's Internet Explorer (there's that imagination at work again). They essentially work the same way, except that they use different semantics.

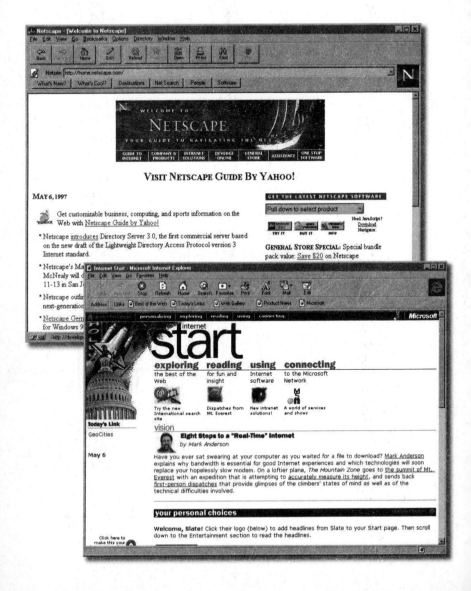

A **home page** is the first page of a site on the World Wide Web, or the page that comes to screen when you open your browser. This can be the one they supply or one you have designed yourself.

Remember, a Web page isn't a home page until you have instructed the browser to use it as a home page. Do this to avoid using the browser-maker's home page which is located on a remote site. Yours, on the other hand, is located on your machine's hard drive, so loading the browser or returning to home will be much, much quicker. It's also personalized with all the things you want in it, instead of being generic and full of features that you don't care about.

This is the ultimate in vanity publishing (although much cheaper) and puts you into a carriage closer to the front of the Web bandwagon.

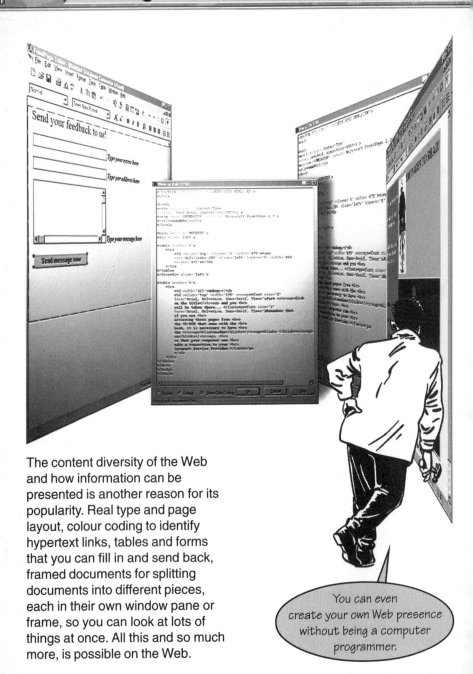

The content diversity of the Web and how information can be presented is another reason for its popularity. Real type and page layout, colour coding to identify hypertext links, tables and forms that you can fill in and send back, framed documents for splitting documents into different pieces, each in their own window pane or frame, so you can look at lots of things at once. All this and so much more, is possible on the Web.

You can even create your own Web presence without being a computer programmer.

Web page creation is now a matter of seconds. Software handles all the coding for you, so that What You See Is What You Get. WYSIWYG is a term originally coined by electronic typesetting system developers to express the accuracy between what something looks like on screen and what it looks like on a piece of film or bromide, and therefore how it will look when it is eventually printed. WYSIWYG systems for the Web present the real content instead of a bunch of HTML codes. They are much easier to work with because someone else has done the code for you.

1. Make sure that you have some content, i.e. something to say that someone else might be interested in. **2.** Create most of the text for your pages in your favourite word processor. Save the documents as plain text (ASCII) or as HTML if your text editor supports this.

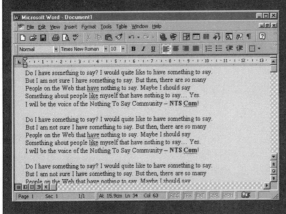

3. Acquire an inexpensive WYSIWYG HTML editor such as Adobe PageMill, Claris HomePage, Netscape Navigator Gold or Symantec VisualPage. All sell for under £100 and can be downloaded from the manufacturers' sites. **4.** Arrange with your ISP for a bit of Web space and check to see if there is any specific title or address you should use on your page to access their WWW server. If you have your own domain address and/or server, you can call your pages whatever you like, providing they are each preceded by the full domain address.

Yes, we do provide Web space for members!

5. Open the Editor and select the option for a "New" page. Go into the "Document Options" or equivalent menu and set a background colour or image for your page. Click at the top of the page and select "Acquire" or "Import" options from a pull-down menu. Select a text document that you have prepared in step 2.

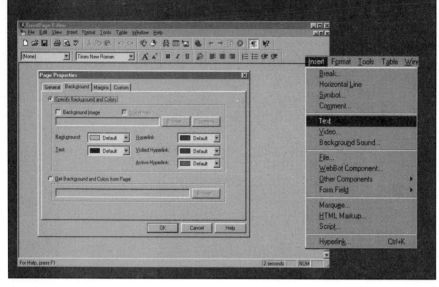

The text is now automatically HTML tagged, if necessary, and placed in your document. If your editor has a "raw" HTML editing page (most do), then you can now take a look at how the program has tagged your text and background colour by selecting this option. In this way you can learn how to write HTML code if you like, but you probably don't, so just ignore that part.

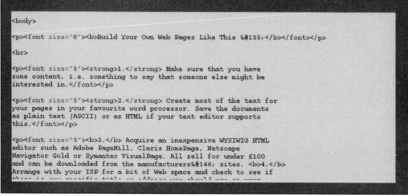

6. Select all of the text in your document and choose a text style, weight, size and colour from the "Style" or equivalent menu. You cannot use specific fonts in an HTML document, only certain styles, weights and sizes of the standard type specifications.

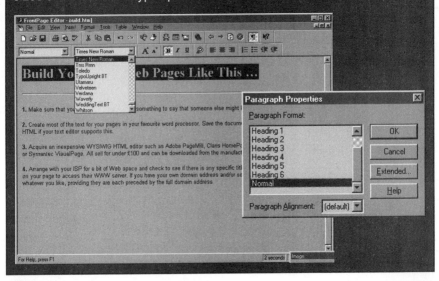

If you want to be annoying, you will select a colour and size that is virtually unreadable against your background colour. Next set the justification Left, Right or Centre by pressing one of the "Align" buttons.

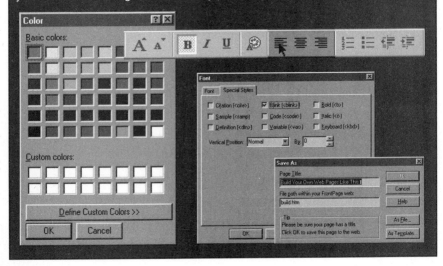

7. Save your document and open up Adobe Photoshop or some other graphic application that can save in a variety of formats. Create some flashy graphics for logos, section headings and a splashy page title.

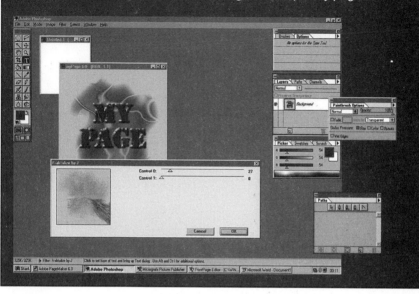

Be completely free with your use of fonts for these graphics. Save each of the elements separately as JPEG files. For Macintosh users, you will have to add the .jpg suffix to each file name. If you already have graphics created for use in your business, you may use these as long as they are in JPEG or GIF format. If not, convert them in Photoshop. Close Photoshop and return to your Editor and Home Page.

8. In your document, click where you want to place a graphic element and select the "Insert Image" or equivalent button. Choose the JPEG or GIF file you wish to insert and this will now be placed in your document. Note how the text moves to make space for the graphic.

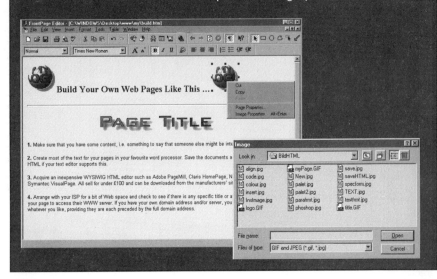

You can play around with this spacing a bit using the "Align" and "Indent" buttons and the Backspace and Return keys, but if you want more precise spacing you will have to learn to code HTML. Now go ahead and place more graphics at various points in your page. When you are reasonably happy with the positioning of everything, press the "View In Browser" button.

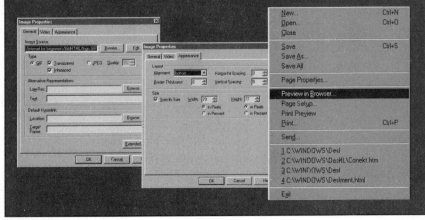

The programme will now locate a Web Browser on your hard disk and open it, displaying your page exactly as people will see it on the Web. You may find that the spacing of things looks different in the Browser than in the Editor.

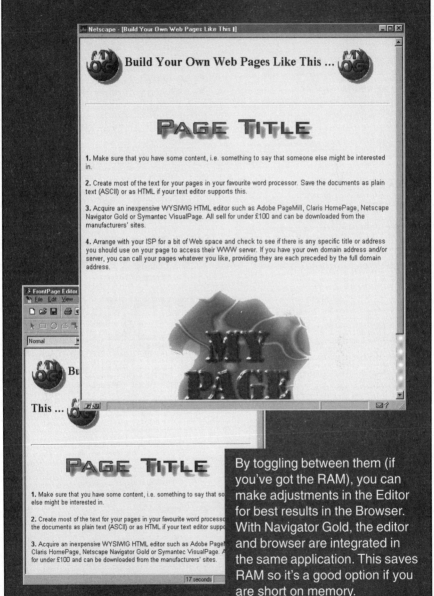

By toggling between them (if you've got the RAM), you can make adjustments in the Editor for best results in the Browser. With Navigator Gold, the editor and browser are integrated in the same application. This saves RAM so it's a good option if you are short on memory.

9. You now have a basic Web page with text and graphics. If you find that your page is very long and takes a bit of scrolling, you can add "Anchors" to parts of the document with links to a Contents section at the beginning. Simply click where you want to place an Anchor, press the "Anchor" button and type in a link name which will be appended to the main file name.

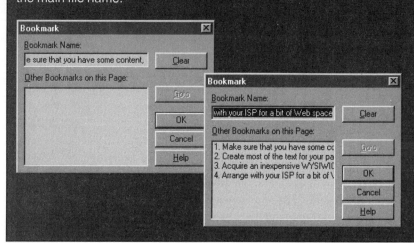

Now go back to the top of the page and type in your Contents section however you please. Set the Type size and Style and Align parameters. Don't worry about colour. With the mouse, define the first selection in your Contents and press the "Link Editor" button.

```
src="file:///D:/Internet%20for%20beginners/BildHTML/myPage.GIF"
width="333" height="333"></font></p>

<p align="center"><font size="2" face="Arial"></font> </p>

<p align="center"><a href="build2.htm"><font size="4"><em><strong>Go
To Next Page</strong></em></font></a></p>
</body>
</html>
```

Type in the name of the Anchor that you wish to attach to this selection. The selection now becomes a Link and will appear underlined in the Link colour that has been chosen in the Document Options window (the default colour is blue, and this is the Web standard). Repeat steps for all Contents topics. Alternatively, graphic elements can be used for the Contents, with the Links created in exactly the same way as above.

Long pages take longer to load than short ones. It is usually preferable to have many short pages rather than one long one with lots of Anchors. This can easily be done by creating a new HTML document for each section of your "Page" and pointing your Contents Links to these pages rather than to different sections of the same page.

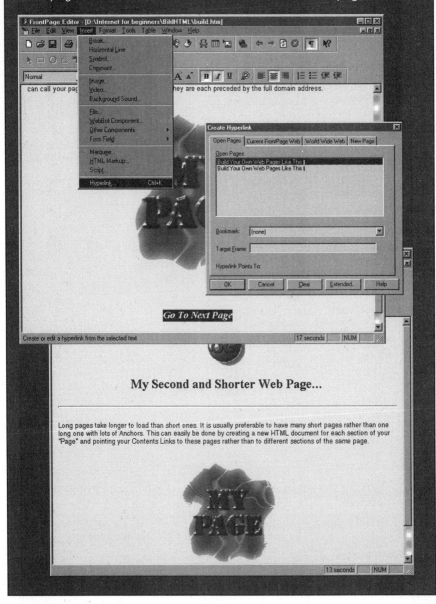

10. Make sure all pages are saved with the proper file names. Remember that any page that you wish to make accessible across the Web must have a full domain address, including the file name.

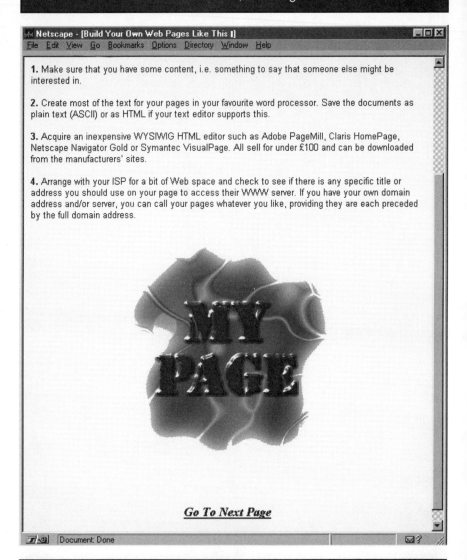

Netscape - [Build Your Own Web Pages Like This I]

File   Edit   View   Go   Bookmarks   Options   Directory   Window   Help

1. Make sure that you have some content, i.e. something to say that someone else might be interested in.

2. Create most of the text for your pages in your favourite word processor. Save the documents as plain text (ASCII) or as HTML if your text editor supports this.

3. Acquire an inexpensive WYSIWIG HTML editor such as Adobe PageMill, Claris HomePage, Netscape Navigator Gold or Symantec VisualPage. All sell for under £100 and can be downloaded from the manufacturers' sites.

4. Arrange with your ISP for a bit of Web space and check to see if there is any specific title or address you should use on your page to access their WWW server. If you have your own domain address and/or server, you can call your pages whatever you like, providing they are each preceded by the full domain address.

Go To Next Page

Document: Done

You have now created a basic page with text, graphics and links. When you become more familiar with HTML and the Web, you can get a bit more adventurous with things like Frames, Tables, QuickTime, ActiveX, Java and RealAudio. Have fun.

Think about it in terms of content and purpose. You can put in as much content as you want, but will it be useful? What kind of response do you want? Think about how your information is organized. Don't have cluttered pages, excess graphics, or forget crucial information like your real-world address and telephone number. Keep your file sizes small.

The Web may be a new publishing medium, but there are many conventions from traditional print that can work on the Web. A table of contents and an index are two. There are more, so look at print equivalents of your material and see what will work. Don't be constrained by the printed page, though. Web publishers can go far beyond the bounds of paper. When in doubt, pinch someone else's idea.

Here is our cut-out-and-keep HTML code for building your home page and linking to other pages on your site.

```
<!DOCTYPE HTML PUBLIC "-//IETF//DTD HTML//EN">
<html>
<head>
<meta http-equiv="Content-Type"
content="text/html; charset=iso-8859-1">
<meta name="GENERATOR" content="MyPages">
<title>Untitled</title>
</head>
<p>Put the title here<br clear="all">
<br clear="all">
Put your text here<br clear="all">
<br clear="all">
<a href="otherpage.htm">
Put a link here</a></p>
</body>
</html>
```

Hypertext links are a doddle to create, and you can link without the permission of the document's owner or creator.

The Web provides no means of controlling the route a reader will take, or of predicting it, although the **route can be traced** ...

Encryption is becoming quite a hot topic as more people use the Internet, and particularly the Web where most content abuse occurs. Encryption converts your file into nonsense that can only be unscrambled with the necessary decryption software. The American government has been particularly sensitive about its having deemed encryption software a weapon.

This had meant that Americans who wanted to develop and sell or publish such software had to register as arms dealers and apply for an export licence!

There are many issues here, most significant of which is freedom of speech. That governments believe they can restrict their citizens or invade their privacy, based on a suspicion of sedition or anti-social behaviour, is scary.

However, if we are to conduct financial transactions on the Internet, some form of security is mandatory. Rest assured that encryption will be a reality, if for no other reason than because it is necessary for business.

If you are concerned about site security, contact CERT. The Computer Emergency Response Team, superheroes in digital tights, investigate security violations and provide a coordination centre for virus administration problems.

The Web is the area of the greatest innovation on the Internet at the moment. Programming languages dedicated to the Web such as Java and ActiveX which can link disparate software components are powerful technologies that can manipulate data via the Web.

If you are interested in Java tools, try www.Gamelan.com, the "official" Java directory.

Browsers can do more than handle diverse data formats including text, images, audio and HTML documents. They can be set up to control how you get information. With server push, the server will send updates to a browser automatically. With client pull, the browser requests the page updates.

Dynamic and prescriptive document creation is possible. If a browser cannot handle a data format when it encounters something new, it can pass the file to a plug-in or viewer. The plug-ins convert the browser into a viewer temporarily, whereas viewers need to be launched as applications. Plug-ins are consequently more common because they're easier, but viewers generally have more features which means you can do more with them.

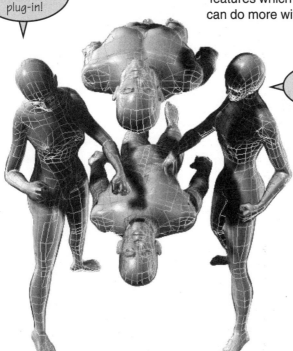

Plug-ins add specific functionality.
Some plug-ins: RealAudio to hear real-time audio from a Web page, QuickTime, ActiveX and ShockWave to access multimedia elements from a Web page.
activeX
RealAudio
real
... the possibilities are endless. (If you want to use snazzy things such as RealAudio, your ISP must run special software on its server.)

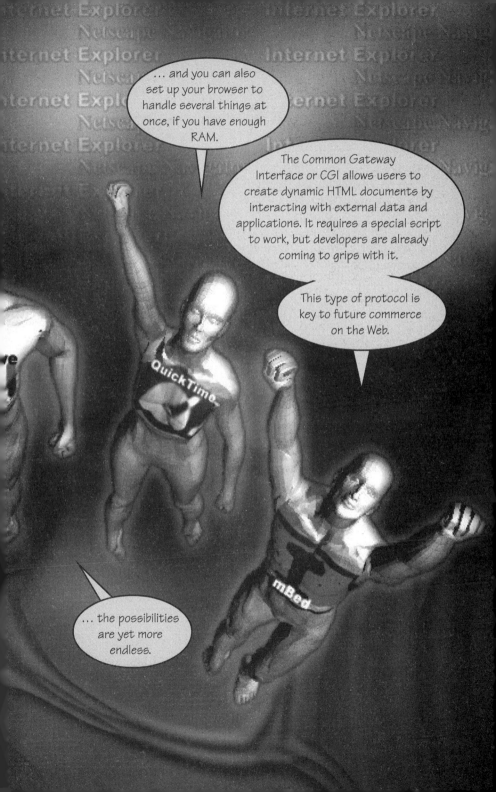

There are three types of search engine on the Web. **Automatic indexes**, **agents**, and **manually configured lists**. Automatic indexes are created by software that trawls through http sites looking for things and adding their vital statistics such as location, title and some text to the database in a keyword-retrievable form. Programs such as InfoSeek, AltaVista and HotBot are in this category, and are not unlike Archie in principle.

Agents do the same sort of thing, but they are live and base their activities on what you tell them to do, performing dedicated searches.
See agentware.com for some of these.

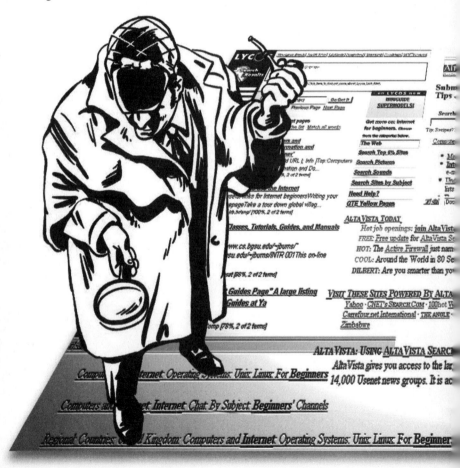

Manually configured directories are sites sorted by topic, machine, date, name and so on, and will generally include some comment on the site. Magellan is one such.

Search engines vary in their suitability for different types of search. They also differ in how well they work and in how specific you need to be to get what you want. Most of them give you a guide to using them and this is well worth following if you plan to spend a lot of time searching.

Lycos and Yahoo search Gopher sites as well as those on the Web. There are also specialist file directories for really obscure and vague searches: TuCows or Stroud, ftp search and Snoopie.

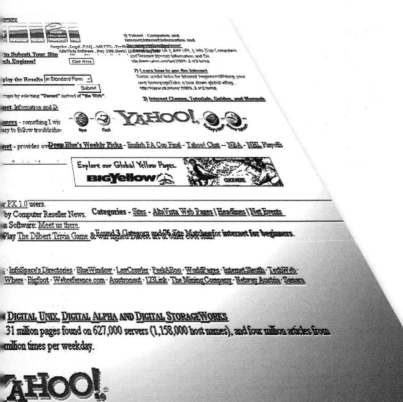

All of this has serious implications for the professional publishing industry, one of the reasons why copyright and liability in the digital world are such a tricky subject.

The Internet, and specifically the Web, is a new publishing medium. This is about much more than gathering research documents from university archives. It is about content forms and means of access on a scale not previously possible.
It is also about content theft and abuse on a scale not previously possible.

And in the digital world, content is anything described in binary code, including music, pictures, statistics, lists, video, cartoons, software, and collections of disparate entities.

The Web is about dynamic information, and its power to shape communications and human knowledge is unprecedented. Yikes!

Unlike the Internet, the Web is also about commerce, another of its distinguishing characteristics, albeit a less beneficent one.

Actually, conventional commerce on the Web has been a bit of a disappointment.

Most of the money earned through a Web presence has been money saved.

Customer services can be conducted via a Web site, with a link to a powerful computer that can provide online technical support by presenting pages from a digital manual, for example.

 structur...
...ommerci...esou...
magazine articles, a
...Way Out of the W
...ed in ...ness Week of M
...s K. Ho's notion of 'Focastin
...The Net Pays Off (Informatic
...d the linkages to suppliers and c
...ning practice.
...he Electric Handshake (Row, D
...nderscore a distinct shift from the
...uilding. Also accessible are relate
...ternet Marketing: Is the Emphas
...and Academy of Managemen
...illusioned by the promises held
...ct sales channel. Prescriptions
...ffer...about the ongoing viab
...ding Back E-Commer
...question: Despite techn
...rs? Besides the two
...that needs to b
...rketp

This isn't a reason to pooh pooh the Web, though. We just haven't figured out how to make it pay yet. Perhaps it is because people are still reluctant to shop via their computer, as there is still a lot of anxiety about making financial transactions over a computer network.

This will fade as people begin to see the similarity between mail order with a credit card, in print or on the phone, and the Web.

We just need to get used to it, to gain the confidence that will turn it from an overhyped media phenomenon into a tangible channel for commerce.

Internet Relay Chat (IRC) is another quite amazing thing you can do on the Internet. IRC is a real-time communications protocol and client/server system that allows you to chat on screen, as long as you have installed the necessary client software. It's offered as part of the online services, or you can go direct. Try the alt.irc newsgroup.

IRC is live, so as soon as you hit the enter key, your typed words will appear on the screens of all participants in the chat session.

Chat and Talk

There are two categories, chat and talk, which differ in the connection method. **Talk** is a direct connection to another person. **Chat** is an indirect connection via a chat room, so that one or many people can be involved in a specific discussion group.

They are private interest areas, already pre-qualified by a person's participation in a given channel.

Group chats often have invited guest speakers who lead the discussion or make themselves available to answer questions. Second- and third-rate pop stars can do this in an effort to be hip and revive a flagging career.

155

Online services are generally the best place to start if you want to get into chat sessions. They have done all the set-up for you, so it's easy. There are various possibilities, including CompuServe and AOL. They share some basic commands and features, but will differ in the specifics.

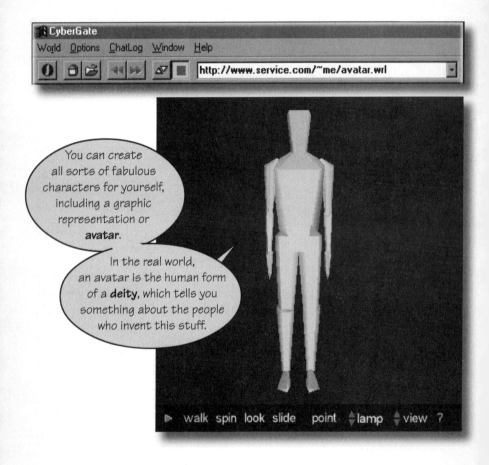

You can also set up a chat session on your Web site, although these can be slow, which defeats the object of spontaneous and lively debates.

IRC chat systems need IRC client software such as Ircle on the Mac or mIRC or PIRCH for Windows. These are quite complex software packages with many features, so if you aren't inclined to wrestle with your computer, use an online service instead. If, however, you like doing digital battle, once you have come to grips with the client software, you will need to connect to an IRC server which will provide you with the necessary channels linking IRC participants.

The server presents you with a list of channels or subject areas which you can extend if you like. Channels change constantly as soon as the conversations peter out. IRC is a very powerful system of communications, and can also be used to send files including software and images.

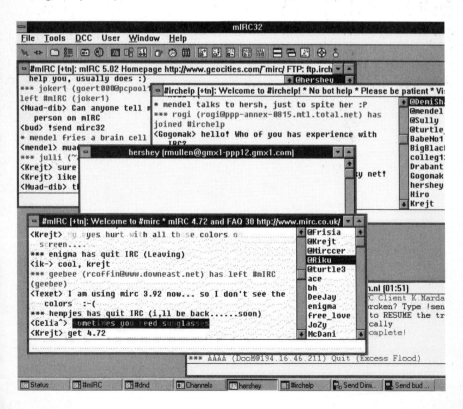

IRC provides a means for spontaneous communication between like-minded people in an open information forum. This makes it ideal for technical support or medical advice to remote locations, because the phone call is local and immediate. It is also good for people in large corporations because it can help build a sense of camaraderie.

With IRC it's a bit like being in a group discussion, or on a mailing list or newsgroup or electronic mail system, except that everything happens immediately. This is why it is so addictive. Invented in 1988, IRC is an evolved version of Unix Talk, a command which was originally used to establish a text link between computers. The command was writ large so that thousands of computers can simultaneously converse.

The two main IRC networks are EFNet and Undernet. EFNet is the more widely used and is generally what is referred to when people talk about IRC. It is also the wilder of the two. Channels for diverse topics from the banal to the frightening allow people to communicate in a completely uninhibited and sometimes thoughtless way.

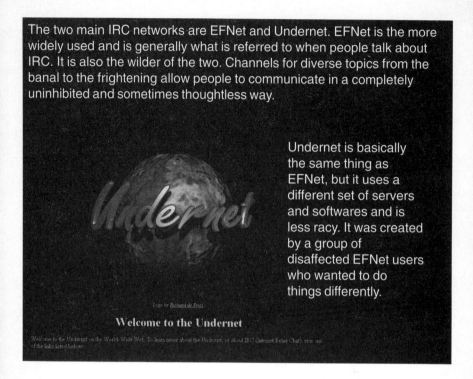

Undernet is basically the same thing as EFNet, but it uses a different set of servers and softwares and is less racy. It was created by a group of disaffected EFNet users who wanted to do things differently.

Logo by Richard de Pres

Welcome to the Undernet

Welcome to the Undernet on the World-Wide Web. To learn more about the Undernet, or about IRC (Internet Relay Chat), visit one of the links listed below:

There is a voice version of this idea, but it's still too clunky and expensive for most people to use: Voice on the Net or VON, Internet Phone, WebTalk or CoolTalk, which is a free product from Netscape. You need to make sure that the person you want to talk to has the same set-up as you, so things are hardly spontaneous. However, technology moves forward at an alarming rate. It is just a matter of time before talking on the Internet will be as easy as email.

Then we can all worry about video on the Internet, but not yet. Video takes a lot of bandwidth and computing power. It will be a while before the current generation of products become good enough for people to use them for much more than emergency or novelty reasons.

> Try CU-SeeMe, invented at Cornell University.

As with all Internet things, remember: time isn't elastic. Socializing via a computer isn't ideal, and analogue partners are rarely understanding about their digital competition, no matter how enlightened you think they are or ought to be. There's also the phone bill to think about, the implications of abstract rather than direct contact with the world, and the fact that the Internet is ultimately a digital mask. The Internet gives you the means with words, sound and images to be someone and something you're not. Bear this in mind when you hop from site to site … it works both ways.

The Internet is a wonderful escape, because you need never see anyone, nor does anyone ever expect anything from you. The Internet creates a universe of activity, yet you can operate within it without having a physical presence. The Internet provides access to a wealth of collective knowledge. Physical isolation and abstracted interaction are key to its joys. But this can also be dangerous, because this is not the real world.

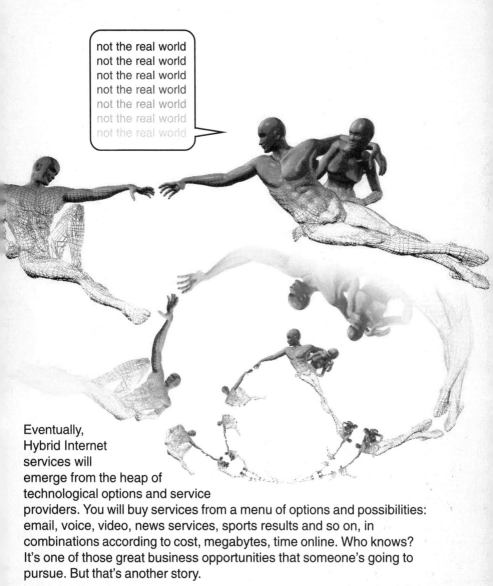

Eventually, Hybrid Internet services will emerge from the heap of technological options and service providers. You will buy services from a menu of options and possibilities: email, voice, video, news services, sports results and so on, in combinations according to cost, megabytes, time online. Who knows? It's one of those great business opportunities that someone's going to pursue. But that's another story.

Internet Bodies and Authorities:

World Wide Web Consortium
[W3C]
http://www.w3.org

Massachusetts Institute of
Technology Laboratory for
Computer Science
545 Technology Square
Cambridge, MA 02139 USA
Telephone: + 1 617 253 2613
Fax: + 1 617 258 5999
admin@w3.org

Institut National de Recherche en
Informatique et en Automatique
Domaine de Voluceau
Rocquencourt
BP 105
78153 Le Chesnay Cedex
France
Telephone: + 33 1 39 63 51 02
Fax: + 33 1 39 63 51 14

Internet Society
http://www.isoc.org

Internet Engineering Task Force
http://www.ietf.org

Internet Assigned Numbers
Authority
http://www.iana.org/iana

Internet Research Task Force
http://www.irtf.org/irtf/

Useful Internet Sites:

http://www.microsoft.com

http://www.apple.com

http://www.dartmouth.edu

http://www.adobe.com

http://www.macromedia.com

ftp://ftp.enterprise.net

ftp://ftp.tidbits.com

http://ftp.cit.cornell.edu

ftp://ftp20.netscape.com/

http://home.netscape.com

http://www.pointcast.com/

http://www.fractal.com

www.wastelands-unlimited.com

http://www.mbed.com

http://www.yahoo.com

http://www.realaudio.com

http://www.synthzone.com

http://www.symantec.com

Understanding why the Internet is so very important is difficult for most of us. After all, it's just a set of computers and wires, just a new-fangled way of sending messages and getting information, right? Well yes, but it's this and so much more besides.

The Internet is about people – an abstraction of their interests that separates them from their associations in the physical world. Its growth and evolution are in the hands of the users. Its power is in how people use it, and people are shaping the Internet's development with every access.

It is a forum for any human interest including the good, the bad and the thoroughly nasty. Somewhere out there is a newsgroup for Hellebore enthusiasts, shoe fetishists and neo-Nazi nitwits. Is this something to encourage or disparage?

The Internet can help preserve communities spread throughout the world, unified only by language, for example. Maybe Esperanto will rise again? Latin? Old Church Gothic? Anyone who wants to resurrect a language can find like-minded souls to share their enthusiasm. Anyone who wants to invent one can do so – look at all those email users who depend on abbreviations and emoticons.

So let's try to "philosophize" the Internet by considering its **pros** and **cons**...

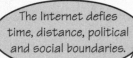

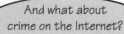

Computing is ultimately vulnerable. A digital device ultimately functions according to how it is programmed, and with each layer of complexity are we building something that might eventually collapse under its own weight?

Who protects our interests on the Internet?

Copyright and information ownership is still a black hole. Digital data that moves around the world passing through server after server: who is the publisher and owner? Who is responsible for that content when it is libellous, seditious?

Some communities are better off virtual than real.

... and some communities are better off real than virtual.

But the Internet creates a chasm between those who have and those who do not have access to electronic tools.

The Information gap gets bigger as computer use spreads.

Information isn't knowledge, but where there is information there is power nonetheless.

The Internet can therefore create huge knowledge gaps. It can undermine the unifying power of broadcast and widely shared media.

Anything you say or do on the Internet will get a response somewhere, somehow. Any kind of virtual community can exist, from amateur poets to religious fundamentalists. Through the process of this communication we are creating a new social fabric, another layer sitting on top of all the other social layers that have been laid down over the centuries. This new layer, like all the others, is informed by what went before. But the Internet is unique because it is not dependent on what went before. This means that we can create an environment for information and knowledge transfer that has no historical baggage, no liabilities and no constraints.

Society is based on the concept of association and acceptance of common assumptions, such as being nice to each other, being considerate, thoughtful, acting in the interests of one another and so on. Most of this has its origins in shared space, common ground that we inhabit collectively, so we have needed a means of holding it all together, unifying it. The basic precepts of social interactions and defined societies have evolved over the centuries through many iterations: families, clans, tribes and so on. The strong families protected the weak ones, who in turn served and defended the interests of their protectors. With each additional layer of complexity came new social and economic rules, new strata of history, new conventions, habits and restrictions. People inhabited larger physical spaces: camps, communes, hamlets, villages, towns, and as their colonies grew so people started bickering about who could have what and go where. The agrarian revolution and the industrial revolution added even more people and complexities. Society built even more complicated controls as industrialization spread. And so the individual was lost in an endless chaos of external artificial structures, organizations and social imperatives. **Until now!**

The Internet and its use is highly personal. It means people can share cultures and concepts of their choice, without obligation or responsibility. There are new realms not bounded by geography or the need for protection. We don't need to share a common structure. We are creating communities of interest that transcend conventional boundaries.

All through history we have created highly complicated, interactive structures. The world has been made up of separate political and national entities providing the socio-economic environment in which we operate. But a digital society in which the channels of interaction are no longer geographically or politically determined is completely unstructured, unconstrained. There is no **locative imperative**.

There are no geographic locations on the Internet, only abstract ones. On the Internet, communities are defined by interest and need, not geography.

On the Internet the individual reigns supreme. A state does not need to exist unless individuals choose to create one. True nationhood defined by collective interests and shared commitment instead of rule-based government is possible on the Internet.

But if there's no possibility of external control, what does that imply for society? Chaos? Freedom? The power to create a utopia? A perfect social, political and legal system? Of course not – there can't ever be any such things, because everything that exists and can be described is ultimately subjective, dependent on its mode of description and interpretation.

So on the Internet we could create a utopia as long as everyone involved agreed?

Well, sort of.

Or we could create a dystopia?

Not likely, unless you want to believe that there **is** a place where everything is as bad as possible, which of course it never really is.

Anyway, both utopia and dystopia are impossible on the Internet because our concept of them is defined in a physical space. The thing that's special about the Internet is the fact that it's non-physical, an abstract world where you can create all sorts of personal and shared environments.

The Internet is a framework, a structure for communication of ideas and of digital commodities and processes. It educates and unifies. It is the means by which communities can define themselves, sharing a part of the digital space unrestrained by geographic or national boundaries. We are creating a new definition of nationhood, where external controls are not necessary or desirable.

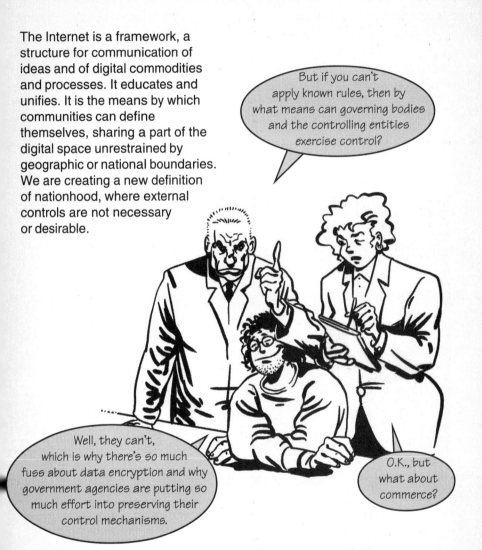

Can we conduct commerce on the Net? Of course we can. Do we want more commerce? Is it really what makes the world turn? Aren't there better ways of getting ourselves fed, housed and clothed? Could the Internet turn into a massive means of bartering? The ultimate black economy of swapsies?

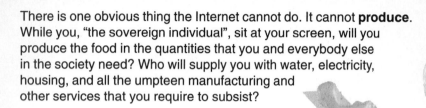

There is one obvious thing the Internet cannot do. It cannot **produce**. While you, "the sovereign individual", sit at your screen, will you produce the food in the quantities that you and everybody else in the society need? Who will supply you with water, electricity, housing, and all the umpteen manufacturing and other services that you require to subsist?

Internet enthusiasts seem to forget that society is not just "there", like a fact of nature, but is produced. Cultures, societies and nation states are not just whimsies of history but the results of production, which is in fact countless human beings working together in large-scale groups.

The Internet is a decentralized model, a world of digital communities where the protocols used define new domains and fiefdoms, where abstract nations can self-select and self-regulate, based on the consensus of the participants.

This might help a utopia or dystopia in abstract, but do we want to do away with central governments? Do we want sovereignties based on specific collective interests? Do we want the individual to reign supreme? If we say "yes" to the freedom, can we cope with what this might unleash?

What happens when all those digital clocks get to 12:59:59 in the year 1999? The Internet will go haywire because of a zillion clocks getting stuck. Don't depend on air traffic control that night! And keep away from trains, traffic lights and tall buildings with electronic lifts. Who knows what will happen!

Acorn 69
Addresses on the Internet 34–41
    see also under Home page;
    Mailing lists
Adobe
    PageMill 132
    PhotoShop 135
Agents *see* Search engines
Algorithm *see under* Routing
ALOHANet: *An early set of networked computers at the University of Hawaii.* 25
AltaVista 148
Amiga 69
Analogue: *An equivalent but not a replica of something else. In computing, it's everything that isn't digital. Analogue computing relies on numbers that represent some measurable thing in the real world, such as a sound wave or frequency of light.*
Analogue signals and modems 47
Anarchie 82
Anchor tag, HTML 126
    creating 138
AOL 71
Apple: *The people who developed the first mass-market graphical computer.* 43
Application software 58–60
Archie 86–9
ARPA: *Advanced Research Projects Agency* 14
ARPANet: *The first internetworked system.* 16
Articles in newsgroups 114
ASCII: *American Standard Code for Information Interchange that uses 8 bits per character. It uses seven bits for the character and one bit for information handling.* 10, 115
    HTML 125
Atari 69
ATM: *Asynchronous Transfer Mode for transmitting scads of data at once, and "the next big thing" in networking. At least it might be.* 49
Attaching files to emails 100
Automatic
    file conversion 115
    indexes *see* Search engines
Avatar 156
Baud: *A unit of signalling speed, which came from inventor Emile Baudot who introduced a five-bit code system in the 19th century.* 52
Binary code: *A numbering system that relies on a mere two digits, unlike decimal which needs 10, or hexadecimal which*

needs 16. 8–10, 99
BinHex: *An encoding system that turns Mac binary files into ASCII.* 100
Bits: *Binary digits, the basic unit of calculation for a computer, the smallest item of information it can cope with, an open or closed switch. Bundles of eight bits are called bytes.* 8, 10
Bookmarks 127
bps 48, 49, 52
Browsers: *Web content viewing software.* 127–9, 145
Browsing
    ftp sites 82
    newsgroups 110
Bulletin board services 23, 70
Byte: *Eight bits, and used to represent a single character.* 10
Cache memory 127
Censorship 71
CERT: *Computer Emergency Response Team.* 144
CGI: *Common Gateway Interface; a bridge created with a little script or set of instructions that sits between http servers and the world beyond.* 147
Charges, ISP 66, 72
Client pull 145
Client-server computing: *A powerful computer providing services to a less powerful one. Big, complicated machines provide services to smaller, easier-to-use machines.* 29
Code *see* ASCII; Binary code; Encryption; Tags, HTML; *see also* Encoding
Compressed/decompressed files: *Data in a compressed file has been specially coded to take less space and so take less time to transmit.* 83
CompuServe 23, 71
Computer
    digital 8
    disk drive, size 56
    linking at ARPA 14
    memory *see* RAM
    organizing 62
    type 54–5, 57
Converting files 115
Country code 34–5
Crackers 32
Crossposting 116
Data encoding, email 99
Datagram *see* Packet
DARPA: Defense Advanced Research Projects Agency 17
Digital: *Of digits, signifying the use of two states: on or off, like your state of mind.*

(cont. next page ...)

Acknowledgements

Laurel Brunner is a freelance consultant and journalist:

Where to begin? With William Eve? With Jonathan Seybold? Yes. Thanks for all the help and all the hassle you gave. Both in equal part contributed to this effort. The one for teaching me not to take life seriously at all, and the other for teaching me that technology is ultimately very dull. What you do with it though, that is the wonder.

Thanks too to a peculiar if somewhat dog-eared family, especially my husband whom I love more than he knows, my sister ditto, and my daughter Hannah who is everything I've ever wanted. And thanks to those who helped with this project, even if it was just to listen to me burble on about it. An especial thanks to my close friends, brave guinea pigs all, who read the manuscript: the brillant but entirely analogue Prince Grenville Griffiths, wonderful Dorothy Hollamby, still an encouragingly unconverted flat-earther, that occasionally courageous Alex Moderski, Derek and Sean at Sahara, and Richard Patterson, the clever clogs technochecks. Hunnybunnies all. These people can all confirm that without Zoran's wonderful images this book was pretty tedious, and for his imagination and pen I thank him. And thanks to Richard Appignanesi for his help.

Finally I'd like to thank all the people in the prepress and graphic arts business who make sense in print of what's in our heads. All of us depend on these people to express and enhance our ideas, and to get the messages through. With their knowledge and experience, information delivery on the Internet can only keep improving.

Zoran Jevtic is a multimedia artist who also illustrated *Cyberspace for Beginners, Baudrillard for Beginners* and *Foucault for Beginners*:

Well, not much space left here, so I'll just express my gratitude to all who are still patient with me and all who helped ... and just for the record: don't blame me or send us hate-mail, I only did the pictures.